P9-CLR-912

Beat the Dealer

BEAT THE DEALER:

A Winning Strategy for the Game of Twenty-One

Edward O. Thorp, Ph.D.

VINTAGE BOOKS
A DIVISION OF RANDOM HOUSE, INC.
NEW YORK

Vintage Books Edition, February 1966

Copyright © 1962, 1966 by Edward O. Thorp

All rights reserved under International and Pan-American Copyright Con-
ventions. Published in the United States by Vintage Books, a division of
Random House, Inc., New York. Distributed in Canada by Random
House of Canada Limited, Toronto. Originally published in hardcover by
Random House, Inc., New York, in 1966. The quotation from Paul
ONeil's article in *Life* Magazine appears courtesy *Life* Magazine © 1964
Time Inc.

Library of Congress Cataloging in Publication Data

Thorp, Edward O.
  Beat the dealer.
  Reprint of the 1966 ed.
  Bibliography: p.
  1. Blackjack (Game) I. Title.
[GV1295.B55T5 1973]   795.4'2   72-8006
ISBN 0-394-70310-3

Manufactured in the United States of America

G 9 8 7 6 5 4 3

This book is dedicated to
my wife VIVIAN
and my children,
RUAN, KAREN and JEFFREY.

Acknowledgments

I am indebted to Roger R. Baldwin, Wilbur E. Cantey, Herbert Maisel, and James P. McDermott for making available the computational details of their work on blackjack and to the M.I.T. Computation Center for making available an IBM 704 computer.

I wish to thank the many friends and colleagues who have made valuable suggestions, particularly Professors Claude E. Shannon, Berthold Schweizer, Abe Sklar, and Elbert Walker. I am indebted to Vivian and James Thorp for the long hours they spent playing the part of "the house." For showing me many of the methods and devices used by casinos in cheating and for giving me a large amount of general information on the world of gambling, I owe a great deal to Michael MacDougall, former special investigator for the Nevada Gaming Control Board, to some of the old-time Nevada "count" players, and to a certain crooked Nevada card mechanic. Conversations with a certain federal investigator have given me a large amount of information about the inside activities and the out-of-state connections of certain Nevada casinos. Last, but not least, I wish to thank the two millionaires who financed the highly successful casino test of my system that is reported in Chapter 5.

The results of the first edition have been sharpened and improved by the extensive researches of Julian Braun of the IBM corporation. He has made most of the calculations for the point-count method and has made numerous detailed and valuable suggestions. I am grateful to him for allowing his work to be incorporated into the second edition.

I particularly wish to thank William E. Walden for the related work he has done with me on Nevada baccarat.

Thanks to Paul O'Neil for the integrity and journalistic clarity with which he portrayed *Beat the Dealer* and its author in *Life* magazine. Thanks also to *Life* for its courageous stand in printing the truth despite hostile Nevada mobsters and politicos.

I wish to thank many readers for their helpful suggestions, ideas, personal experiences, and testimonials, and for proving the book again and again in the casinos.

Finally, thanks to the readers of the first edition of *Beat the Dealer* who, in their enthusiasm, bought so many copies that they put it on the national best-seller list.

"There is a tide in the affairs of men, which, taken at the flood, leads on to fortune. . . ."

—SHAKESPEARE (*Julius Caesar*)

Contents

Beat the Dealer

I

Introduction

The game of blackjack, or twenty-one, is one of the world's most widely played gambling games. In the United States it is played in the state of Nevada, in Jefferson Parish near New Orleans, in the Galveston area, on and off in Hot Springs, Arkansas, in White Sulphur Springs, West Virginia, and in homes and private clubs throughout the country. Blackjack can be played in Puerto Rico, Aruba, Panama, the Grand Bahamas, and other spots in the Caribbean. There is blackjack in Europe at the Lido casino in Venice, on the Isle of Man, and in London.* Manila, in the Philippine Islands, and the Portuguese colony of Macao, near Hong Kong, also have casinos which feature blackjack.

In England, blackjack is known as "van-john" and in Australia, as "pontoon." Both of these are corruptions of the French term *vingt-et-un*. In Germany it is called *Ein-*

* As of this writing, many forms of gambling are legal in England. A number of the large London gaming clubs have blackjack rules that are essentially the same as those in Las Vegas. The winning strategies in this book apply.

und-Zwanzig or *Achtzehn-und-Drei*. Although the name varies, the game is essentially the same.

In the modern casino game of blackjack, the player can gain a consistent advantage over the house by using the strategy presented in this book. Based on the mathematical theory of probability, this strategy was worked out with an electronic computer by the author and others. It is fortunate and perhaps surprising that the system reduces to a few simple charts that can be understood and memorized by the average player. In addition, the system lends itself to the rapid play usually encountered in casinos.

The rules of blackjack vary somewhat from casino to casino. These variations, based on my studies of many casinos, are listed in Table 9.2. The table shows how these rules variations affect the player's chances and enables him to compare any two casinos and decide in which one to play.

No system can win when confronted with the chronic disease of gambling games: cheating. Blackjack gives the dealer an excellent opportunity to cheat. Aside from not playing at all, the only sure protection seems to be to have the services of a card expert. But, by taking the precautions described in Chapter 10, the average player can protect himself sufficiently in most situations.

In the following pages we begin by outlining and discussing the rules of the game and then proceed step-by-step to advance the reader to any level of playing proficiency he desires. The first step is to learn what we shall call the "basic strategy": a simple set of rules which tell the player when to draw or stand, when to double down, and when to split a pair. With the basic strategy alone the player has the slight *advantage* of 0.1 per cent in most Las Vegas casinos. Blackjack is the only casino gambling game today where *you* can consistently have the edge. Other published strategies for blackjack commonly give the player disadvantages ranging from 2 to 5 per cent. The first substantially correct version of the basic strategy was discovered by Baldwin *et al.* and published in [2].* There were slight inaccuracies both in this version and in the improved version published in the first edition of *Beat the Dealer*. The correct version of the strategy for one deck and a certain set of casino rules appears in Chapter 3. It was calculated by Julian Braun. In casinos with favorable rules the basic strategy actually gives the player a larger edge over the house. In casinos with unfavorable rules, the player may have a slight disadvantage (up to 0.5 per cent or so). Even so, he is generally better off than in any other casino game, including craps.

The basic strategy does not involve counting cards. However, after mastering the basic strategy, the reader will learn a simple modification, using a card-counting system, that identifies many situations in which he has an advantage over the casino of more than 3 per cent. Most people who are advised to count cards say, "But I can't keep track of all the cards in the deck. I can't even remember telephone numbers." They may be surprised to learn that they must count only four cards (per deck used by the dealer) —the Fives—and that this additional information, combined with minor strategy changes, is enough to give the player a comfortable 3 per cent edge!

The player who is willing and able to count more than four cards can go on to more sophisticated strategies. First, there is the powerful new Thorp point-count system. This method was perfected by several people after the first edition of *Beat the Dealer* was published. It has proven very effective against assorted casino countermeasures. In particular it is effective and easy to use against several decks. It is as simple as the famous Goren point count in bridge. Every card is counted +1, 0, or −1 as it is seen. You simply need to keep track of the *total* number of points you have seen (thus you remember *one number only*). The

* Numbers in [ ] indicate references listed on pp. 205–9.

point-count method is effective because it takes into consideration every card the player sees. This allows him to identify nearly half of all situations as favorable to himself. In fact, half the time he has a slight edge in the one-deck game as soon as he sees a single card!

The Ten-count method was presented in detail in the first edition. It was used so successfully by thousands of readers that the Las Vegas casinos, for the first time in history, changed the rules of blackjack. [34]. (The change failed and was dropped. When I wrote the book I foresaw the change and explained in Chapter 8 [of the first edition], Rules Variations, how to continue winning. The casino operators apparently only managed to read as far as Chapter 5.)

For skeptics who do not believe a theory until they see it work, in Chapter 5 there is an account of the author's original test of the Ten-count method in Nevada. Backed by $10,000, which was lent by two millionaires interested in making a profit, I purposely played very conservatively for about thirty hours. At the end of this time, the millionaires' $10,000 had increased to over $20,000. As we became known, it became harder and harder to get the casinos to play a "nice" game. The tactics they used included refusing to give us a private table, shuffling every hand or two, switching dealers in and out, changing decks constantly (one casino switched in four new decks in five minutes), and refusing to sell us large-denomination chips. One casino even introduced a cheating dealer when we sat down to play.

Despite these annoyances, we were still able to get games whenever we wanted them. We finally quit because the millionaires had bigger business elsewhere, because my teaching duties required me to, and because the system had been sufficiently tested.

We think that this book will pay for itself and for the time spent reading it many times over. Anyone who frequents the gaming tables or who plays for stakes at home should be handsomely rewarded for his trouble. We hope also that some of the aura of superstition and mystery surrounding games of chance will be dispelled for the reader as we study blackjack together.

2

The Rules of Blackjack

The first step in learning the game of blackjack is to master the rules—with emphasis on the word "master." Even knowing the exact meaning of the rules is not enough. The reader must be able to understand the effect of each rule and of each possible variation. Both experienced players and beginners should study this chapter.

Each casino has a set of blackjack rules which agree with those of other casinos on the main points but which usually differ in details. Later in this book we shall analyze the effects of these variations; but first, for simplicity, we consider a typical set of rules. A set that is common, yet by no means universal, is listed below.

Number of Players

A blackjack game has a dealer and from one to seven players. We will see later that, generally speaking, the fewer the number of players at a table, the better it is for the player.

The Pack

One ordinary 52-card pack is commonly used. However more and more casinos are going over to two and even four packs shuffled together, in an effort to make card counting more difficult.* It turns out that an increase in the number of packs cuts the player's advantage slightly. (In Puerto Rico two decks are generally used, and in London four decks dealt from a shoe are common.)

The Deal

Before play begins, the cards are shuffled by the dealer and cut by a player. Next, a card is "burned" (placed face up on the bottom of the deck). The burned card may or may not be shown. The dealer then deals two cards to himself and to each of the players. Players get both cards face down. The dealer receives one card face up and one card face down. The two cards of the player and the "down" card of the dealer are called "hole cards."

Some casinos deal the player's hole cards face up. This is the practice in Puerto Rico. This is very convenient for players who count cards. On the other hand, seeing the player's cards in no way helps the dealer if, as is usually the case in casinos, he must act according to fixed rules. Later we shall see that about half the time the absence of the one burned card is enough to give the player a slight edge over the house. (This is not true when two or more decks are used.)

Betting

The players place all bets except insurance (discussed subsequently) before any cards are dealt. The house establishes a minimum bet and a maximum bet. The minimum

* In Nevada the multipack dealing devices, which are more and more common, have come to be known informally as "perfesser stoppers." (See the UPI story by Harold Drake, "Prof Who Beats Vegas Heads for UCI.")

bet is usually between 25¢ and $5 and the maximum bet, between $100 and $500.

Our winning strategies involve varying the size of the player's bet. The player places larger bets in favorable situations and smaller ones in unfavorable situations.

The size of the minimum bet is of greatest interest to the player with a small amount of capital. The size of the maximum bet is of interest to the player with a large amount of capital because it limits the rate at which he can win. (In Puerto Rico, a $1 minimum and a $50 maximum are common. In London a minimum of from 5s. to £1—approximately 70¢ to $2.80—and a maximum of £50—about $140—are common.)

Numerical Value of the Cards, Hard and Soft Hands

The player can choose either 1 or 11 as the value of an Ace. The numerical value of a face card is 10, and the numerical value of the other cards is simply their face value. We call a hand "soft" if it contains an Ace and that Ace can be counted as 11 without causing the total to exceed 21; we call all other hands "hard." Since there are two possible totals for a soft hand, we shall define the total for a soft hand as the number obtained by counting the Ace as 11.

The distinction between hard and soft hands is important. We shall see that the best strategy for a player with a soft hand of a certain total usually differs sharply from his strategy with a hard hand of the same total.

Object of the Player

Each player tries to obtain a total that is greater than that of the dealer but that does not exceed 21.

Naturals

If the first two cards dealt either to the player or to the dealer consist of an Ace and a 10-value card, they

constitute what we shall call a *"natural"* or *"blackjack."*
If a player has a natural and the dealer does not, the
player receives 1.5 times his original bet from the dealer.
If a player does not have a natural and the dealer does,
the player loses his original bet. If both player and dealer
have naturals, no money changes hands.

In 1964 automatic blackjack machines were introduced into northern Nevada which paid 2 to 1 for an untied player natural. We analyze these machines in Chapter 9.

The Draw

The draw starts at the left of the dealer and proceeds
in clockwise fashion. A player looks at his hole cards and
may elect to "stand" (draw no additional cards); otherwise,
he can request additional cards from the dealer, which are
dealt face up, one at a time.

If the player "busts" (goes over 21), he immediately
turns up his hole cards and pays his bet to the dealer. After
each player has drawn his cards, the dealer turns up his
hole card. If his total is 16 or less, he must draw a card
and continue to draw cards until his total is 17 or more, at
which point he must stand. If the dealer receives an Ace,
and if counting it as 11 would bring his total to 17 or more
without exceeding 21, then he must count the Ace as 11
and stand.

Many casinos alter this rule for soft hands so that the
dealer draws on soft 17 or less and stands on soft 18 or
more; in this way they gain a small advantage. Some casinos
gain still more by other variations of this type.

It is common practice for the player to request additional cards from the dealer either by saying "Hit" or
"Hit me" or simply by scratching the felt table top with
his cards. To refuse additional cards the player places his
hole cards face down and may also say "Stand" or put his
cards under his bet. It is considered bad form for the player

to touch the bet itself after the deal has begun. One reason for this is that players have been known to attempt, by sleight of hand, to alter their bet after seeing the dealer's up card.

The Settlement

If the player does not go over 21 and the dealer does, the player wins an amount equal to his original bet. If neither player nor dealer busts, the person with the higher total wins an amount equal to the original bet of the player. If dealer and player have the same total, not exceeding 21, no money changes hands.

A player-dealer tie is called a "push." When there is a push, the dealer removes the player's cards without touching his bet. This often seems to be confusing, so to bring the "push" forcibly to the player's attention, dealers sometimes hold the player's cards face up and strike the table a couple of times before removing them.

In some games the dealer takes *all* ties. This gives him a horrible 9 per cent edge. Avoid such games.

If ties are a standoff, one might think that, except for the effect of naturals, the game is even if the player uses precisely the same strategy as the dealer. However it has been observed that the player who uses the strategy of the dealer loses at an average rate of 5 to 6 per cent.* The reason for this is that if the player busts, he loses his bet to the

---

* In *Scarne's Complete Guide to Gambling* [58] it is claimed on pages 19 and 317 that the book's author was the first person to calculate the bank's favorable percentage at blackjack. On page 317 it is also asserted that this percentage appears in the book for the first time anywhere. The bank's favorable percentage seems to mean (see pages 18, 19, 687) the average rate (i.e., percentage of the total amount bet) at which the player loses in the long run.

On page 326 of [58] it is remarked that it is not feasible to figure the exact percentage against individual players because their strategies differ widely. Also on page 326, full-deck composition is assumed for the analysis. Then on page 328 it is further assumed that the player follows the same rules (i.e., *strategy*, as the following sentences show) as the dealer. Thus the book seems in reality to be presenting the solution to the problem: If the player follows the same strategy as the dealer, i.e., stands on all totals of 17 or more, draws on all totals of

dealer, even though the dealer may later bust also. Thus the case wherein both the player and dealer bust is an example of a "tie" that is won by the dealer.

Splitting Pairs

If the player's hole cards are numerically identical, they are called a pair. He may choose to turn them face up and to treat them as the initial cards in two separate "twin" hands. This is known as "splitting a pair." The original bet goes on one of the split cards and an equal amount is bet on the other card. The player automatically receives a second card face down on each of the split cards. He then plays his twin hands, one at a time, as though they were ordinary hands, with the following exceptions. In the case of split Aces, the player receives only one card on each Ace. Further, if a face card or Ten falls on one of the split Aces, the hand is not counted as a natural but only as ordinary 21. Similarly, if a player splits a pair of face cards or Tens and then draws an Ace, it counts only as an ordinary 21. If a player splits a pair and receives a third card of the same value, he is not permitted to split again.

Aces are the best pair to split. The temporary Las Vegas rules changes, now off again, forbade splitting Aces. The first automatic blackjack machines introduced into Nevada do not allow pair splitting.

Doubling Down

After looking at his hole cards a player may elect to double his bet and draw one, and only one, more card. This strategy is known as "doubling down." A player who doubles down turns up his hole cards and receives his third card face down. A player who splits any pair except

16 or less, and does not split pairs or double down, what is his average rate of loss?

To set the record straight we mention that Baldwin, Cantey, Maisel, and McDermott published the solution to this problem several years prior to the Scarne book, first in a mathematical paper [2, p. 439] and later in their book [3, p. 27].

*Aces may, after receiving an additional card on each of
the split cards, double down on one or both of his twin
hands.*

In Puerto Rico doubling down is permitted on a total
of 11 only. Some Nevada casinos, particularly in the Reno
and Lake Tahoe areas, allow doubling down only on totals
of 10 and 11. The same was true of the first automatic
blackjack machines. The temporary Las Vegas rules
changes, now off again, also restricted doubling down to
totals of hard 11. This was the only rules change besides
the restriction on splitting Aces mentioned above. Restrictions on doubling down tend to increase the house advantage.

Insurance

*If the dealer's up card is an Ace, an additional wager
is allowed before the draw. After checking his hole cards,
a player may put up an additional side bet equal at most
to half his original bet. After the player has decided
whether or not to do this, the dealer checks his hole card.
If the dealer has a natural, the side bet wins twice its
amount. If the dealer does not have a natural, the side bet
is lost and the play continues. The original bet is settled in
the usual way, regardless of the side bet.*

Suppose, for instance, that the player makes the side
bet, and that the dealer has a natural and the player does
not. The player then loses his original bet but wins the
same amount back on the side bet, for no net loss or gain.
This is why the side bet is referred to as "insurance." Many
of the casinos in northern Nevada do not allow insurance,
nor do the automatic blackjack machines.

Customs and Practices

There are customs and practices connected with the
game of blackjack which are not to be thought of as part
of the rules. They vary erratically from casino to casino,
sometimes in the same casino on different shifts, and some-

times even among dealers on the same shift. (Nevada casinos generally are open continuously, night and day, and there are therefore three shifts of employees. In Puerto Rico the casinos are generally open from about 8 P.M. to 4 A.M., so there is only one shift.) These customs and practices will have little bearing on the basic strategy of Chapter 3 but will be of interest in connection with the winning strategies to be discussed subsequently.

Shuffling. It is a custom that the dealer can shuffle at any time between hands. Also the dealer shuffles in the midst of the play of a hand if the deck is exhausted. A dealer who shuffles in the *midst* of the play of a hand when unused cards remain is probably a cheat. The player may request a shuffle between hands. Some dealers comply and some refuse.

We shall refer to the practice of unnecessarily frequent shuffling by the dealer as "shuffle up."

Shills. A shill is a house employee who bets money and pretends to be a player in order to attract customers or to stimulate play. Shills may or may not be used in a given casino at a given time.

Shills generally follow "shill rules"; i.e., they never double down, split pairs, or insure, and they stand on hard totals of 12 or more. They often follow the dealer's rules for drawing or standing on soft totals. If the shill does not follow a fixed strategy he may be helping the dealer and/or house to cheat the players (see our later discussion of "anchor men").

New decks. The player by custom, but not necessarily by law, is supposed to be able to request a new deck whenever he wishes. Generally new decks are first spread face down. Among other things, this gives the dealer a chance to check the backs of the cards for imperfections that in turn could be used by the player to identify cards when they are face down. Then the cards are spread face up. This gives the player a chance to see that no cards have been removed from or added to the deck(s).

3

The Basic Strategy

During one Christmas vacation, my wife and I decided to relax from my teaching duties at the University of California at Los Angeles by spending a few days in Las Vegas. We both had been there before, but we were not gamblers. We enjoy the shows, the luxurious low-cost meals, and in season, the swimming pools.

Before we took the trip, Professor Sorgenfrey of U.C.L.A. told me of a recent article in one of the mathematics journals [2]. The article described a strategy for playing blackjack that allegedly limited the house to the tiny overall edge of 0.62 per cent.* Because this figure is so nearly even, and so much better for the player than in any other casino game, I wrote the strategy on a little card and carried it on our trip.

When I arrived at the blackjack tables, I purchased

* Mr. Wilbert E. Cantey has told us that an error in arithmetic, discovered after [2] and [3] were published, shows that the figure given for the house advantage should have been 0.32 per cent, rather than 0.62 per cent. The correct figure for their strategy is a *player* advantage of 0.09 per cent.

ten silver dollars. I did not expect to win but wanted to see how long my stack would last, as well as to try out this strategy "under fire."

In a few moments the slowness of my play and the little card in my palm had attracted amused bystanders. The dealer could not conceal his scorn for one more "system" player. These sentiments were soon laced with pity when these people saw the way I played. Who split a pair of lowly Eights—and doubled the amount of money being risked—when the dealer's up card was the powerful Ace? Had anyone ever seen a player who doubled down on (*A,2*) against a Five or who chose to stand on a piteous 12 (hard) against a Four?

To add to this poor beginner's misery, the dealer was having a very strong run of luck. Every player at the table was losing heavily. Surely my ten "crumbs" would soon be swept away. Or would they? Somehow these weird plays kept turning out right. As other players lost heaps of chips, my little stack held. It even inched up once. After twenty minutes most of it was still there. Beginner's luck.

Then a strange thing happened. I was dealt (*A,2*). I drew a Two, and then a Three. I now had (*A,2,2,3*), a soft 18. The dealer had a Nine up, but he might have had 19. Only a fool would draw again and risk the destruction of such a good hand. I consulted my card and drew. With no little satisfaction and several "tsk-tsk's," the amused onlookers saw me draw a Six. Hard 14! "Serves me right." I drew an Ace which gave me hard 15. Tough luck; I drew again. A six! I now held (*A,2,2,3,6,A,6*) or seven-card 21. This is an event so rare that it only happens once per several thousand hands.

After a moment of shock, some of the bystanders said I had a $25 bonus coming. The dealer said "No"—it was only paid at a few places in Reno. I was unaware of such a bonus. But I thought it might be amusing to create the impression that I had sacrificed my soft 18 because I foresaw the seven-card 21. "And who knows, they might even pay me." Of course they did not. But the amusement and patronizing attitude of some bystanders changed to respect, to attentiveness, and even to goose pimples.

After another fifteen minutes—and after the obliteration by the dealer of all my fellow players—I was behind a total of eight and one-half silver dollars and decided to stop. But the atmosphere of ignorance and superstition that pervaded my little experience securely planted in my mind the suggestion that even "good" players did not know the fundamentals of this game. There might be a way to beat it.*

When I returned home, I began an intensive study of the game. I was convinced at once that a winning system could be devised with the help of a high-speed electronic calculator. As the first step in finding such a system, I used an IBM 704 computer to improve the strategy discussed in the above episode. It is this revised version—which I call the "basic strategy"—that you will learn in this chapter. It is the foundation for the winning strategies of later chapters. Calculations show that in a typical casino the player who uses the correct basic strategy has an edge of 0.12 per cent over the house. In some casinos the player actually has a narrow advantage of as much as 0.6 per cent. In casinos with the most adverse rules the player has a disadvantage of less than 1 per cent. Against some of the automatic blackjack machines, the basic-strategy player should *theoretically* have an advantage of 1.6 per cent and be able to win consistently. For details, see Chapter 9.

Time and time again you will need to use this basic strategy while "waiting" for more favorable betting situations to arise. It must be so completely memorized that any decision it calls for can be made without hesitation.

---

* There will be numerous anecdotes and incidents concerning our strategies in actual play. They are here to make things "come alive." The reader is cautioned that one or a few incidents should not *in themselves* be construed as supporting evidence for the system.

The Player's Decisions

As we saw in the last chapter, the game begins with certain preliminaries. When the players are seated, the deck is shuffled by the dealer and cut by a player, and the dealer burns a card. After the players have placed their bets on the table in front of them, the dealer gives two cards to each player and to himself. As mentioned previously, one of the dealer's cards is up and the other down.

At this point the player must make a number of decisions. The principal ones are whether to split a pair, if he has one; whether to double down or not; and whether to stand or draw. In general, what the player should do depends on the cards he holds, on the dealer's up card, and on any other cards the player may have seen. However, in this chapter the player completely ignores all cards he has seen except his own hole cards and the dealer's up card. The basic strategy, given in this chapter, is the *best possible* way to play with this information alone. Later, we shall improve our strategies by using the knowledge gained both from the player's seeing which cards were consumed on previous rounds of play and also from his seeing, on the current round of play, exposed cards other than his own hole cards and the dealer's up card.

The player's key decisions (pair splitting, doubling down, standing or drawing) *and the order in which he makes them* are illustrated in Figure 3.1.

The Basic Strategy for Drawing or Standing

In the great majority of hands the player will neither split a pair nor double down. Thus his decision is reduced to whether he should draw or stand. Since this decision is the simplest and most important part of the strategy, we shall learn it first, temporarily neglecting the possibilities of pair splitting and doubling down.

With a hard hand, consult Table 3.1 in order to de-

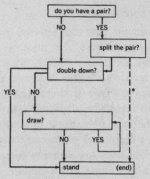

FIGURE 3.1. *The Player's Key Decisions.*

* Recall that when a pair of Aces are split, you are obliged to stand after being dealt one card on each Ace.

cide whether to stand on your current total or draw one or more additional cards in an effort to improve your hand.

Notice that Table 3.1 recommends drawing on all hard totals of 11 or less. This is reasonable because a player who does this cannot bust and must increase his total.

TABLE 3.1. *Drawing or Standing with Hard Hands.*

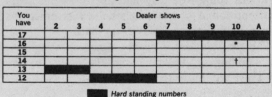

You have	Dealer shows										
	2	3	4	5	6	7	8	9	10	A
17										
16										*
15										
14										†
13										
12										

▬ Hard standing numbers

* Holding hard 16, draw if you hold two cards, namely **(10,6)** or **(9,7)**, and stand if you hold three or more cards, for example, **(6,4,4,2)**.
† Stand holding **(7,7)** against **10**.

Table 3.1 is a pictorial list of "hard standing numbers." The hard standing number for a certain dealer's up card is simply the smallest total you stand on against that up card. For example, if the dealer shows a Seven, then Table 3.1 shows the standing number is 17. This is your goal with a hard hand. You stand on hard totals of 17 or more. You draw with hard totals of 16 or less. When the dealer shows a Six as an up card, the standing number drops to 12! Now you stand on 12 or more and draw on 11 or less.

The person who is comfortable with the basic strategy can add the refinements noted. They happen to be for a dealer's up card of Ten. The refinement for totals of hard 16 against a Ten actually considers cards in addition to the player's hole cards. This anticipates later results.

Notice also that if you stand on a given total against a dealer's given up card, you also stand on all higher totals against that up card. Similarly, if you draw on a given total against a given up card, you also draw to all lower totals against that up card.

TABLE 3.2. Drawing or Standing with Soft Hands.

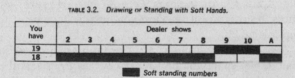

Soft standing numbers

When your hand is soft, use Table 3.2 in order to decide whether to draw or stand. Tables 3.1 and 3.2 are read in the same way. However, when we compare them, we see that drawing is recommended for much higher totals with soft hands than with hard hands. Part of the reason for this difference will be clear from the following argument. Remember we saw that a player with a hard total of 11 or less has nothing to lose by drawing one or more card. Similarly, a player with a soft total of 16 or less has nothing to lose. Since his hand is soft, he cannot bust by drawing a card because if it puts him over 21 when he continues to count the Ace as 11, he automatically counts it as 1 instead. This reduction of 10 in his total will keep the player from busting no matter which card was drawn. If an Ace was drawn, it can be counted as 1, if necessary, and any other card will have a numerical value of 10 or less.

Since the player with a soft total of 16 or less cannot bust by drawing one more card, he cannot make his total poorer. This is because all final, or "standing," totals of 16 or less are equivalent. If you stand and the dealer busts, you win the same amount no matter what your total is. Whether it is 16 or less than 16 makes no difference. If you stand on 16 or less and the dealer does not bust, then by the rules he must have ended up with a total between 17 and 21. Thus he automatically beats all totals of 16 and under. Therefore, if you draw to soft 16 or less, you cannot harm yourself. In fact, you may even be able to help yourself. For example, on holding $(A,5)$, you improve your chances to tie or win if the card you draw is any one of the group $A,2,3,4,5$; on holding $(A,2,A)$, you improve your chances to tie or win if the card you draw is any one of the group $3,4,5,6,7$.

When drawing to a soft 17, there is a small possibility of loss. If you stand and the dealer also has 17, you will tie him and thus avoid losing your bet. However, if you draw to soft 17, you may convert your hand into a hard hand that totals less than 17. If you then stand on this, you are worse off than before, for the dealer may end up with exactly 17 and now you lose, whereas you would have tied. If you draw to this hard hand, you may bust and lose at once. For example, with $(A,3,3)$=soft 17, suppose a Five is drawn to make $(A,3,3,5)$=hard 12. If the dealer shows a Five, Table 3.4 recommends standing. If the dealer shows an Ace, the table recommends drawing. If a Ten is drawn, we reach $(A,3,3,5,10)$=22 (even counting the Ace as one) and bust.

Despite this chance of making your hand poorer by drawing to a soft 17, calculations show that this risk is more than offset by the possibility of improving your hand. Thus, with $(A,6)$, you may draw an $A,2,3,$ or $4,$ all of which im-

The Basic Strategy

prove your hand. Even if you

you do not bust. You still have anoth

with which to try for a good total.

It sometimes takes a little will power to

instructions. More than once I have been confront

heart-stoppers like this. I was playing a "big-money" ga

in a certain Nevada casino. By the card-counting methods

of later chapters, I knew that I had a 5 per cent edge on

the next round of play. Therefore, I had placed the maxi-

mum bet of $500. The dealer's up card was a 7. I was

dealt *(A,6)*, a soft 17. Since the remaining cards in the

deck consisted largely of Tens, I was fairly certain that

the dealer had 17. Since there were only four cards that

would help me—the *A,2,3,4*—and five that would hurt

me—the *5,6,7,8,9*, I was reluctant to draw and was inclined

to play for a tie. Nevertheless, I gritted my teeth and drew

once, receiving an *8*. I now held hard 15. I held my breath

and drew again; this time I received an Ace. I now held

hard 16. Resignedly, I drew again, receiving—to my amaze-

ment a *3*. I now decided to stand with my hard 19. When

the dealer exposed his hand, to my surprise he held what

happened to be the only Ace yet unaccounted for (one had

already appeared on an earlier round of play). According

to the rules of the game he was required to stand. The basic

strategy not only produced the one line of play that could

save the $500, it doubled the money besides.

We see from Table 3.2 that there are minimum stand-

ing numbers for soft hands similar to those for hard hands.

Thus you should draw if your soft total is less than the soft

standing number given for the current up card of the dealer,

and stand if your soft total is greater than or equal to this

standing number. The reader who practices with the basic

strategy will soon know the standing numbers well enough

to dispense with Tables 3.1 and 3.2.

Suppose now that you go into a casino to practice

using the standing numbers. You never double down, never

do? Surprisingly
ut 2 per cent. Your
er than the methods
world's foremost card

Down

hich is next in importance,
s hard doubling down. It is
pro   to postpone memorizing the
soft-doub   es until after pair splitting has
been learned.   pleteness, we shall also discuss
soft doubling down

As indicated in Figure 3.1, the decision about whether
or not to double down must be made *before* that about
drawing versus standing. This decision is made by using
Table 3.3. The possible up cards of the dealer are again
listed across the top of the table, and the player's totals
are listed in the column on the left. In order to decide
whether to double down, first see if your total appears in
the column on the left. If it does not appear, you should
not double down; instead, proceed to the next decision,
whether to draw or stand. If your total does appear, run
down the column below the dealer's up card until you
reach the row in which your total appears on the left. If
the square at this location is shaded, double down. Note
that the table has two parts. One part is for soft hands
only; the other is for hard hands only.

To illustrate the use of Table 3.3, suppose that the
dealer shows a *3* and you have been dealt *(A,6)*, or soft 17.
On locating the appropriate square you find that it is
shaded. Therefore you double down.

There are several things to notice in Table 3.3. First,
there is no total on which the player doubles down regardless of whether it is hard or soft. Second, hard doubling
down is done only on totals of 11 or less, and soft doubling

draw a 5,6,7,8,9, or 10.
follow these
with
23
if you wish

down is done only on totals of 13 or more. Soft doubling down on a total of 12 is sometimes better than drawing. But soft 12 means a pair of Aces. It is much better to split the Aces instead of doubling down with them.

Observe that the player always doubles down on hard 11. With hard 10, the player doubles down except against an Ace or a Ten. Hard 10 is a less favorable total than hard 11, except when an Ace is drawn, because the total the player obtains when doubling down on hard 10 is one less than the total that he would have obtained by doubling down on hard 11. Hard 9 is even less favorable than hard 10, and with hard 8 the player rarely doubles down. In fact, the situations where you double down with hard 8 are so rare, and the gains are so slight, that you can neglect them with practically no loss.

TABLE 3.3.   *Doubling Down.*

Soft Doubling

You have	Dealer shows				
	2	3	4	5	6
A,7					
A,6					
A,5					
A,4					
A,3					
A,2					
A,A*					

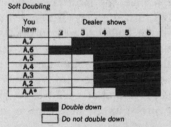

■ Double down
□ Do not double down

*Double down with (A,A) only if Aces cannot be split.

Hard Doubling

You have	Dealer shows									
	2	3	4	5	6	7	8	9	10	A
11										
10										
9										
8				*	*					

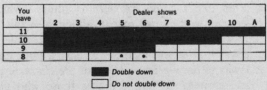

■ Double down
□ Do not double down

*Double down except with (6,2).

A conspicuous feature of the table is that soft doubling down is never recommended against *7,8,9,10,* or *A*.

It is hard to explain the doubling-down strategies without using mathematics. But experience in actual play soon engraves them on the memory. I always remember to double down on soft 13 against a Five because of a hand I played at the Silver Slipper in Las Vegas. On this occasion, my friends and I had gone to see whether this casino would continue to play when we began to win substantial amounts. I was varying my bets from $1 to $10. (A variation of $1 to $3 would be wiser at present, now that thousands of readers of *Beat the Dealer* have inflicted bloody losses on the casinos.) Because I had frequently bet only $1, we agreed that I was not to raise my bets above $10—to do so would attract attention. However, a juicy situation arose (a 6 per cent advantage). I could not resist! I shoved out $30. To my satisfaction the dealer's up card turned out to be a Five, the most favorable card for the player. Confidently I turned up my *(A,2)* hole cards and doubled my bet. I did not bother to look at the down card that was dealt to me because I expected the dealer to have a Ten down and then to draw another card, busting himself. To my horror the dealer's hole card was a Four. He drew the expected Ten for a total of 19. I was resigned to a loss when the dealer turned up my hole card to settle the bet. It was a Seven!

There was a strange expression on the dealer's face. Luck by itself was one thing, but my huge bet in advance made it seem like I could foretell the future (which I could, of course, to a limited extent, although in this case I was quite wrong about the details). What the dealer did not realize was that he was as lucky to have a Four underneath as I was to draw a Seven. One of the characteristics of the basic strategy is that it makes those who use it considerably "luckier" than the average player. In this instance my "luck" proved embarrassing.

Once you have mastered the strategy for *hard* doubling, you further cut the casino's edge to less than 1 per cent.

The Basic Strategy for Splitting Pairs

After memorizing the strategy for drawing and standing and for hard doubling (soft doubling too, if the rest is easy), you are ready to add pair splitting to your repertoire. The detailed pair-splitting strategy will be described, followed by a simple way to learn it.

If you have a pair, Figure 3.1 shows that the first decision you have to make, before both doubling down and drawing or standing, is whether or not to split it. You can decide this by using Table 3.4. In that table the possible up cards of the dealer are listed in a row across the top and the possible pairs of the player are listed in the column on the left. If you have a pair, run down the column below the dealer's up card until you get to the row labeled with your pair. If the square at this location is blank, do not split your pair. Proceed immediately to Table 3.3. If the square is shaded, first split your pair and then go on to Table 3.3. If you have no pair, as is the case about six times out of seven, skip Table 3.4 altogether and go directly to Table 3.3.

If Table 3.4 seems imposing, you may replace it by an *approximate* set of rules. They are: always split Aces and Eights; never split Fours, Fives, or Tens; split the other pairs when the dealer shows 2 through 7. The heavy lines in Table 3.4 indicate this set of rules. Notice that the approximation introduces only five errors. Some of these errors are quite large, but because the situations arise infrequently, the effect is to add only 0.13 per cent to the overall house advantage. Once you have learned to use these approximate pair-splitting rules with your doubling-down and standing-versus-drawing strategy, you are ready to learn the pair-splitting strategy in detail.

The one hundred pieces of information in Table 3.4

are easier to learn by visualizing the arrangement of the squares. For example, the information in forty of the squares is contained in the rule "Always split Aces and Eights, never split Fives and Tens." There are "reasons" for these rules that may help you to retain them.* Aces should be split because there is a very good chance of getting a winning hand—even 21—with each of the new hands, whereas the original hand (A,A) is only fair for doubling down or for drawing or standing.

TABLE 3.4. Pair Splitting.

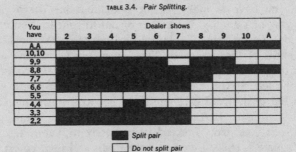

If the dealer has a 7,8,9,10, or A up, Eights should be split, not so much because a good total will be obtained with each new hand, but rather because 16 is, in general, a bad total to hold. The reason that 16 is unfavorable is this. When the dealer's up card is 7 or higher, he is not likely to bust; and if he does not bust, he is sure to beat 16. Thus, the splitting of Eights against 7 through A "breaks up" a bad hand.

It turns out that the new hands are not very unfavorable (in fact, they have about an average chance of winning), and even though you are staking more money, your

* These "reasons" are only a very crude picture of the actual state of affairs. The precise situation is given in the Appendix. We give "reasons" here to help you fix the rules in your mind without having to worry about involved mathematical points. Those who need further assistance might consult [14].

net loss is greatly reduced. When the dealer shows a *2,3,4,5,* or *6,* the splitting of Eights gains in two ways. First, a bad hand is replaced by two average ones. Second, the dealer's chance of busting is quite high with these up cards, and thus there is an advantage in getting more money onto the table.

The splitting of Tens is unfavorable because it generally replaces one very good hand (20) by two that are generally just a little better than average. Splitting Fives is not advantageous because it replaces a total that is good to double down on or good to draw to, by what are likely to be two poor hands.

Notice that the strategy is the same for Twos, Threes, and Sixes—split only if the dealer shows any card from *2* through *7.*

The strategy for Sevens stuck in my mind simply because Sevens are split when the dealer shows any card from *2* through *8,* and *8* is one more than *7.* With Nines, split when the dealer shows *2* through *9* (Nines-9 should be easy to remember) with this exception: do not split Nines when the dealer shows a *7.* Here is a way of remembering that exception. Two Nines give a total of *18.* If the dealer shows a *7,* a total of *17* is much more likely than usual for him (see Appendix Table 1, Dealer's Probabilities); it pays to stand, in the hope of beating him.

Tables 3.1-3.4 are presented as a group in Table 3.5. The format of the miniaturized summary of the basic strategy in Table 3.5 is also used in our winning strategies.

At first glance, Table 3.5 may seem to contain some ambiguities. For example, holding *(A,6)* against a dealer's up card of *4,* should the player double down or merely draw? According to Figure 3.1, the player should consider doubling down first, and Table 3.5 recommends doubling down, so he doubles down.

A copy of Table 3.5 appears at the end of the book in a detachable form for reference. The table may be re-

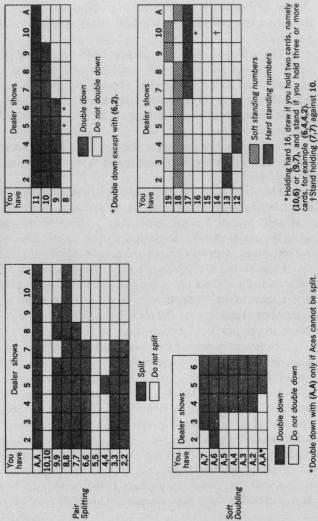

TABLE 3.5. A Complete Miniature Version of the Basic Strategy.

Pair Splitting

You have	Dealer shows									
	2	3	4	5	6	7	8	9	10	A

■ Split   □ Do not split

* Double down with (A,A) only if Aces cannot be split.

Soft Doubling

You have	Dealer shows				
	2	3	4	5	6
A,7					
A,6					
A,5					
A,4					
A,3					
A,2					
A,A*					

■ Double down   □ Do not double down

Hard Doubling

You have	Dealer shows									
	2	3	4	5	6	7	8	9	10	A
11										
10										
9										
8					*	*				

■ Double down   □ Do not double down

* Double down except with (6,2).

Standing Numbers

You have	Dealer shows									
	2	3	4	5	6	7	8	9	10	A
19										
18										
17									*	
16									†	
15										
14										
13										
12										

▨ Soft standing numbers   ■ Hard standing numbers

* Holding hard 16, draw if you hold two cards, namely (10,6) or (9,7), and stand if you hold three or more cards, for example (6,4,4,2).
† Stand holding (7,7) against 10.

moved from the book and used while playing. As you become more expert you will consult the card less frequently and finally not at all.

What to Expect When Using the Basic Strategy

You are now familiar enough with the basic strategy to try it out in actual play. If a casino is not available and you play at home, be sure that the set of casino rules we have adopted are in force. This will mean a considerably different procedure from that usually employed in a home game, but perhaps your friends will go along in the interest of learning something new about blackjack.

The following data may encourage you to try the basic strategy at the casinos in spite of the fact that when you use it you are still, in general, simply playing about even with the house. Table 3.6 describes the possible outcomes that can be expected if 100 hands (generally from thirty minutes to one and one half hours of playing time, depending on the speed of the dealer and the number of players at the table) are played at $1 per hand, and also if 1,000 hands (generally from five to fifteen hours of playing time, depending on conditions) are played at $1 per hand. If the amount bet per hand is different, just multiply all dollar values by the appropriate number. For example, if you bet $5 per hand, multiply by 5; if you bet 50¢ per hand, multiply by 0.50 (or divide by 2). The average gain after one thousand $1 bets is $1. After one hundred $1 bets, the average gain is 10¢. Thus we regard the basic strategy as essentially even: no real advantage for either side.

Baldwin *et al.* [3] report the results in Table 3.7 with their strategy (it is essentially the same as the basic strategy).

The number of hands played in each group is near enough to 1,000 so that if we pretend the number of hands played is 1,000 each time in Table 3.7, we can use the

TABLE 3.6. *Results Using the Basic Strategy.*
If 100 hands are played at $1 per hand—

approximate per cent of time that	the result is*	
	between	and
0.01	—$19.9	below
0.1	— 14.9	—$19.9
2.1	— 9.9	— 14.9
13.6	— 4.9	— 4.9
34.1	0.1	— 4.9
34.1	5.1	0.1
13.6	10.1	5.1
2.1	15.1	10.1
0.1	20.1	15.1
0.01	above	20.1

If 1,000 hands are played at $1 per hand—

approximate per cent of time that	the result is*	
	between	and
0.01	—$62.2	below
0.1	— 46.4	—$62.2
2.1	— 30.6	— 46.4
13.6	— 14.8	— 30.6
34.1	1.0	— 14.8
34.1	16.8	1.0
13.6	32.6	16.8
2.1	48.4	32.6
0.1	64.2	48.4
0.01	above	64.2

* Negative numbers indicate losses.

TABLE 3.7. *Results of Baldwin, et al.*

Number of hands played	Gain
930	$38.50
770	—56.00
1140	— 4.50
690	— 4.00
3530	—$26.00

second part of Table 3.6 for a rough check of the results of Table 3.7. Everything is normal except for the swing of −$56. This swing, if it is not the result of causes other than chance, is a rare event. Table 3.6 tells us that if 1,000 hands are played, the chance of a swing of −$56 or more is less than 0.1 per cent. With a smaller number of hands, in this case 770, the chance of such a swing is even less. In fact, calculations show that if 770 hands are played at $1 per hand, the probability that the player will lose $56 or more turns out to be approximately 0.01 per cent; that is, the odds against this are about 10,000 to 1.

Comparison with House Percentage Against Other Blackjack Strategies and in Other Games

We remarked earlier that the basic strategy is better than other blackjack strategies and that it is also better than any published strategy for any other gambling game. Tables 3.8 and 3.9 illustrate how much better it is.

TABLE 3.8. *The Basic Strategy Compared with Other Blackjack Strategies.*

Blackjack strategy	Player's advantage (in per cent)
basic	+0.1 is typical; ranges roughly from −1 to +1
card experts [8]	−3.2
mimic the dealer	−5.7
typical casino player	−2.00 to −15.00
never bust	−6.0 (estimated)

Some Common Blackjack Errors

The basic strategy for blackjack was first published (with a few insignificant* errors) by Baldwin *et al.* [2] four years before this book was begun. Nevertheless blackjack strategies containing gross errors continue to appear.†

* We call them insignificant because they cost the player on the average a mere 0.04 per cent of his action.

† In this section we are comparing the basic strategy with only those strategies in which complete deck composition is assumed, that is, strategies which do not count cards.

TABLE 3.9. *The Basic Strategy Compared with Best Play in Other Casino Games.*

Game	Player's advantage (best play) (in per cent)
blackjack, basic strategy	+0.13; ranges roughly from −1 to +1
craps	−1.40 (may drop as low as −0.6; see [80])
roulette (Europe)	−1.35
roulette (United States)	−2.70 to −5.26
Nevada baccarat	−1.06 (banker); see [70] −1.24 (player); see [70]
faro*	−1.52 is average; ranges from −30.0 to 0; see [80]

* Card counters who consistently make even-money bets (0 per cent edge) are frowned upon by the operators of this vanishing game. The variation in advantage which is given assumes that the player is aware of the case keeper's record of cards played.

In the discussion to follow, we shall formulate experiments to demonstrate several of the more obvious of these errors. Some of the experiments will take the reader less than an hour. Each reveals the error in one of the commonly recommended systems by comparing with it a feature of the basic strategy.

The experiments should convince anyone who tries them that the basic strategy is correct on these points and that the other strategies are seriously in error. Study of these experiments should enable you to formulate your own experiments for testing the gross differences between the basic strategy and any other strategy. We can, in principle, test *any* discrepancy, not merely the large ones; in the case of close decisions, however, the experiments are unpleasantly long.

Tables referred to in the rest of this chapter are in the Appendix. There is no need now to refer to or understand these tables. The important thing is to get the idea of how to check a strategy by experiment.

First Experiment: Drawing Versus Standing Holding Hard 16 Against an Ace

Table 2a shows us that the player who draws rather than stands on hard 16, when the dealer has an Ace showing, gains an average of 14.6 per cent in such situations. Put another way, to stand rather than draw on hard 16 *costs* the player an average of 14.6 per cent. The following experiment is designed to verify this. Remove an Ace from a complete deck and place it face up on the table. This represents the dealer's up card. Next, write the number 16 on a card or paper and place it in front of yourself. This represents your hard total.

Of course this does not correspond exactly to the real situation. In a game the cards that the player actually has drawn to make up his total of hard 16 will alter the advantage in drawing. Conceivably, if enough small cards are used to comprise the total, it may even be wise to stand. For example, consider the very close decision as to whether to stand or draw when holding hard 16 and the dealer's up card is a Ten. According to Table 2a, drawing is favored over standing for an *average* gain of 2.9 per cent. But when the player's hard 16 total is composed of (4, 4, 4, 4), the precise figure is 6.382 in favor of standing, according to J. H. Braun.

The objection to the use of a paper total in our experiment is answered as follows. A player could replace our experiment by one in which he played a real game of blackjack and kept a record of the results of standing versus drawing in this situation. His average long-run result would be within a few tenths of a per cent of the 14.6 per cent figure based on paper totals. Therefore much time and trouble can be saved by a paper-total experiment. The same considerations apply to the other experiments.

Let's return to our experiment. Shuffle the deck and deal 200 dealer "hands" as follows. Assume you stand on

16 and deal a card to the dealer (his hole card). If he gets
a natural, discard the 10-value card and do not record the
result. We do this because the question of whether or not
to draw on hard 16 arises only if the dealer has already
checked and found he has no natural. If the hole card is
not a Ten, continue dealing until the dealer either busts
or achieves a total, soft or hard, of 17 or more. If the
dealer busts, you win. If he does not bust, you lose. Record
the result. Discard the used cards and deal another hand.
When 100 "hands" are dealt in this fashion the player will
win, on an average, about 17 of the hands and lose the
rest. This follows from the assertion of Table 3, that the
player who stands on 16 when the dealer shows an Ace
loses at the rate of 66 per cent.

Next, deal 200 hands as follows. Give the dealer one
card (his hole card). If it is a Ten, discard it and deal
another card, for the same reasons as before. Now assume
you draw exactly one card to a total of 16. If you bust, you
lose. Discard the card and record the loss. If you do not
bust you have a hard total between 17 and 21. Stop drawing to your own hand and, if necessary, proceed to give the
dealer further cards until he either busts or gets a total of
17 or more. Record whether you won, tied, or lost, and
continue.

Your percentage of "wins" should be figured as the
number of wins plus one half of the ties (to tie every hand,
for example, would be substantially the same as winning
half and losing half, for no net gain). In this part of the
experiment, the average number of "wins" per 100 hands
should be 24.3. Thus, with 200 hands the average separa-
tion between the two ways of playing hard 16 against an
Ace will be 2 × (24.3 − 17.0) or 14.6 hands. In each
part of the experiment, however, there will be chance deviations from the cited average totals. In fact, 1 time in 50,
standing on hard 16 against an Ace will produce better
results, over 200 hands, than drawing.

Second Experiment: Doubling Down on Hard 10 Against an Ace

This experiment is conducted in much the same way as the previous one. Select as hole cards $(8,2)$ for the maximum error of 6.1 per cent, in order to shorten the experiment. This figure of 6.1 per cent is obtained from Table 4j, where we see that, holding $(8,2)$ versus an Ace, if we simply draw until we reach a suitable total, in the long run we win about 8.6 per cent of our bet. However, if we double down we win only 2.5 per cent of our original bet in the long run. The difference is 6.1 per cent. Play about 400 hands in which you double down. Afterward, subtract the number of hands lost from the number of hands won. Then double this number to take into account your doubled bet on the double-down hands. This is your total profit in the 400 hands by doubling down against the Ace. Remember as before to disregard all dealer naturals in your tally. If the dealer has a Ten under, give him another hole card.

Next, play 400 hands in which you follow the correct drawing and standing strategy versus an Ace (Table 3.5). Your wins minus your losses give your profit for the 400 hands. On the average, in 400 hands you will have an excess of wins over losses of about 17.2 hands with drawing and standing. With doubling down, you will have an average excess of wins over losses of 5.0 hands.

Third Experiment: Splitting a Pair of Sixes Against a Five

According to Table 4f, the gain here by splitting rather than standing is $17.2 + 10.2$ or 27.4 per cent. If you stand, you have a net loss of 10.2 units per 100 bets. If you split, your 100 hands become 200 and you will win about 17.2 more of those 200 hands than you lose. You have an average net gain of 27.4 units per 100 original hands by splitting rather than standing. Fifty original hands of each type should be decisive.

Mimicking the Dealer

To quote Baldwin *et al.* [2, p. 439], "The player who mimics the dealer, drawing to 16 or less, standing on 17 or more, never doubling down or splitting pairs, has an expectation of —0.056." That is, the dealer has a 5.6 per cent edge.

Let us illustrate the use of Table 1 by computing a figure for the player who mimics the dealer. First notice that when the player follows these rules, the game is symmetric except for two situations. If both the dealer and player bust, the dealer wins. Count the dealer as a bust if he would have busted supposing that, although the player busts and bets are settled, the dealer plays out his hand anyway. This favors the dealer. The edge it gives him is the probability that both dealer and player bust. Since the dealer and player are assumed to be using the same strategies, Table 1 (Dealer's Probabilities) applies to both of them. The overall probability of each busting is therefore 0.2836 and (assuming stochastic independence, not strictly valid but good in this instance to a high degree of approximation when the deck is nearly complete) the probability of both busting is 0.2836 × 0.2836, or 8.04 per cent, in favor of the dealer, as a result of this factor. The second nonsymmetry in the game is the fact that the player wins 1.5 units when he has a natural and the dealer does not. The dealer, on the other hand, only wins one unit from the player when he has a natural and the player does not. This happens 4.68 per cent of the time for each side, so the player gains one half that amount, or 2.34 per cent from this factor. Thus, the net dealer's edge is (8.07 − 2.34), or 5.73 per cent.

The Player Who Never Busts

Another interesting figure to calculate is the advantage which the casino has against a player who never draws to a possible bust hand. First we note that this means the player's hard standing numbers are all 12. However, the soft standing numbers are not determined. Thus the problem is meaningless as stated. Since it is unanswerable as it stands, we assume soft standing numbers of 17 and proceed. As we pointed out earlier, common sense dictates that the soft standing number should always be at least 17. We know that 18 is always better than 17, so 17 gives the player a greater average rate of loss than he would have with soft standing numbers of 18. We will call a player using this curious strategy "conservative."

We assert that the true figure for the house advantage against a conservative player is between 5 and 8 per cent. Our evidence comes from three sources. First, we ran an experiment in which six groups of 100 hands each were played with the conservative strategy. The number of player units lost ranged from 13 to 2, with an average of 7. The agreement with our figure of 5 to 8 per cent is good. Since the figure of 600 hands was selected in advance and not influenced by the results of the early hands, standard formulas from the mathematical theory of probability apply to this data. We conclude that the true figure for the house advantage almost certainly lies between 3 and 11 per cent. Second, we ran a hand calculation (which is comparatively easy because of the low hard standing numbers) that proved that the true figure was well below 10 per cent. Third and best, Baldwin and his coauthors give a figure of 4.25 per cent for the house advantage against a player who stands on hard 12, never doubles down, and splits Aces and Eights only. (They fail to specify the soft standing numbers.) It can be shown that splitting Aces and Eights adds less than 1 per cent to the player's advantage. The correction, if any, for different soft standing numbers is also, overall, of the order of 1 or 2 per cent. Thus the true figure estimated from this source is between 5 or 6 per cent and 8 per cent.

The Man Who Trimmed His Barber

The disadvantages of such conservative play are amusingly illustrated by the experience of "the man who trimmed his barber," my friend Professor John Blattner of the mathematics department of San Fernando Valley State College.*

Blattner and his barber fell to talking about blackjack one day. When Blattner told the barber of his friend who wrote a book on how to beat blackjack consistently, the barber scoffed. "Why that's easy," said he. "Anyone can win by just refusing to go bust (standing on hard 12 always). Blattner tried in vain to convince the barber that he was wrong. Eventually the barber touted Blattner into a little game after closing hours. Blattner brought $160. At $5 and $10 a hand, the barber quickly lost an equal amount. He constantly exclaimed that Blattner was the luckiest man he ever saw. After losing the $160, he refused to quit. He demanded the chance to get his money back. They played on at $20 a hand. When he was behind $1,200, the barber's luck turned. He won back $300 of this loss. Then it was all over. He fell behind $1,500 and quit.

The barber still believes Blattner is lucky. He delayed paying his loss. Finally he decided to give Blattner free haircuts. After a year of these he cried that hard times were upon him and went back to charging Blattner. (The barber insists that he will pay Blattner some day.) Question: Did Blattner trim his barber or didn't he?

* There is a bit of mathematical irony in this story, as we shall see. As background for the nonmathematical reader, we mention Bertrand Russell's famous paradox. Suppose that a barber in a certain town trims the hair of all those persons, and only those persons, who do not trim their own hair. (We assume that a person's hair is always trimmed by the same person.) Who trims the barber's hair? If someone else trims the barber's hair, then it must be the barber who trims the barber's hair. Impossible! If the barber trims his own hair, then it cannot be the barber who trims the barber's hair. Impossible! Who trims the barber's hair?

4

A Winning Strategy

Gamblers soon learned through experience that games of chance could be run in such a way that a certain "percentage" favored one side at the expense of the other side. That is, if a game was played a sufficient number of times (the "long run"), the winnings of the favored side would generally be near a certain fixed percentage of the total amount of all bets placed by the opponent. The modern gambling casino takes the side in its games that has proven in practice to be favorable. If necessary, the casino alters the rules of the game so that the casino advantage is sufficient to cover expenses and also yield a desirable rate of profit on the capital that the owners have invested.

The total amount of bets placed is called "action." For example, if I place bets of $3, $2, and $11, I have "$16 worth of action." A player who has a certain amount of capital can generally get many times that amount in action before ultimately losing his capital to the house. This contributes greatly to the excitement of gambling.

Failure of the Popular Gambling Systems

There have been many attempts to overcome the casino advantage. A frequent approach has been to vary the amount that is bet from play to play according to various methods, some of which are simple and some of which are very complex. By way of illustration, in the Small Martingale, better known as the "doubling-up," system, the player makes an initial bet of, say, $1. If he loses, he bets $2. Then he wagers $4, $8, $16, and so on, doubling the bet each time *until* he wins. Then the process is repeated starting with $1 again. The bet placed following a string of losses equals the entire amount lost in the string, *plus* one. A winning bet either is a $1 bet, or has been placed after a string of losses. Thus each win results in a net profit of $1, counting from just after the last win, and the player keeps winning a dollar every few bets. However, this system has a flaw. The casino always sets a limit to the amount that may be bet. Suppose the limit is $500 and we have started by betting $1. If there is a string of nine losses ($1, $2, $4, $8, $16, $32, $64, $128, $256), the next bet called for by the "doubling-up" system is $512, and this bet is not permitted.

It seemed in practice that, with this limit on bets, the casino won the same percentage of the action it normally wins, even though a player was using the doubling-up system. Thus the doubling-up system provided no advantage whatsoever to the player. The other complicated betting schemes all seemed to have the same flaw. It was no surprise, then, when it was later proven, by the mathematical theory of probability, that for most of the standard gambling games no betting scheme can ever be devised that will have the slightest effect upon the casino's long-run advantage.

The games for which this is an established fact include those games that mathematicians call "independent trials processes." (Craps and roulette are such games.*) What this means is that each play of the game is uninfluenced by past outcomes and, in turn, has no influence on future outcomes. For example, suppose we shuffle a deck of cards and draw one card, which happens to be the Four of Spades. We now return this card to the deck and shuffle *thoroughly*. If we draw one card again, the chance that it will be the Four of Spades is no greater than and no less than the chance of its being any one of the other 51 cards. This fact has made popular the phrase "The cards have no memory."

The Importance of the Dependence of Trials in Blackjack

In contrast to the previous situation, in casino black-jack the cards do have a memory! What happens in one round of play may influence what happens both later in that round and in succeeding rounds. Blackjack, therefore, may be exempt from the mathematical arguments which rule out favorable gambling systems for independent trials games.

Suppose, for example, that the four Aces appear on the first round that is dealt from a fresh, thoroughly shuffled deck. After that round is over, the cards are placed face up on the bottom of the deck and the second round is dealt from the remaining unused cards. Now on the second round no Aces can appear; there will be no blackjacks, no soft hands, and no splitting of Aces (splitting Aces is highly favorable to the player). This situation of having no Aces in play (which is, on the average, almost 3 per cent against the player as we shall see later) continues in succeeding rounds until the deck is reshuffled and the Aces are brought back into play.

A few years ago one casino made a practice of remov-

* We assume "perfect" dice and a "perfect" roulette wheel. For an interesting account of attempts to beat biased roulette wheels, see Wilson [80].

ing four Tens and a Nine from the deck. From our calculations, we know this added 2.5 per cent to their advantage. This deception was spotted by the Nevada Gaming Control Board and the casino was brought to trial. Eventually the casino's license was revoked. However, there was one ironic sidelight to the trial. The casino operators were practical men through and through and not at all theoreticians. They knew that their short deck helped them but they did not know how much. Thus they had no answer for the damning assertion of an expert witness that they were putting the player not at a 2.5 per cent disadvantage but at a 25 per cent disadvantage!

The Use of Favorable Situations

The winning strategies to be given in this book depend largely on the fact that, as the composition of a deck changes during play, the advantage in blackjack will shift back and forth between player and casino. The advantage often ranges beyond 10 per cent for one side or the other and on occasions even reaches 100 per cent. We watch the cards that are used up on the first round of play. The fact that these cards are now missing from the deck will, in general, shift the house advantage up or down on the hands that will be dealt on the second round from the now depleted deck.

As successive rounds continue to be dealt from the increasingly depleted deck, and the advantage shifts back and forth between player and house, we make large bets when the player has the advantage and very small bets when the house has the advantage. The result is that the player usually wins a majority of his large favorable bets, and although he generally loses a majority of his small unfavorable bets, he has a considerable net profit.

Here is one very special example of a favorable situation that would be uncovered by a careful count of the cards that are played. Suppose you are playing the dealer "head on"; this means that you are the only player at the table. Suppose also that you have been keeping careful track of the cards played and you know that the unplayed cards, from which the next round will be dealt, consist precisely of two Sevens and four Eights.* How much should you bet? Answer: Place the maximum bet the casino will allow. Even borrow money if you have to, for you are certain to win if you simply stand on the two cards you will be dealt.

Here is the analysis. If you stand on your two cards, you do not bust and are temporarily safe. When the dealer picks up his hand, he finds either (7,7), (7,8), or (8,8). Since his total is below 17, he must draw. If he holds (7,7), there are no Sevens left so he will draw an Eight and bust. If he holds (7,8) or (8,8) he will bust if he draws either a Seven or an Eight—the only choices. Thus the dealer busts and you win.

This brings us to the central problem that I had to solve in analyzing the game of blackjack: How can a player evaluate the depleted deck in general to determine whether or not it is favorable, and if it is favorable, precisely how much so? This problem was solved** by asking the IBM 704 high-speed electronic computer a series of questions. The first question was: Suppose blackjack is played with a deck from which only the four Aces are removed. What is the best possible strategy for the player to follow and what is the house (or player) advantage? In other words, the computer was to do exactly the same thing it had done in finding the basic

* The essential thing is that there be at least three Eights and at most two Sevens actually *available for play*. For example, if the casino does not deal the last card (a frequent practice), two Sevens and three Eights would not work in this example.

** It was solved by me to a high degree of approximation. More exact recalculations were made later by Julian Braun of the IBM corporation. Throughout this revised edition we have used his figures in place of our original ones, wherever possible.

strategy, with one difference. It had to solve the problem with a deck from which the four Aces were missing.

The result was noteworthy. When playing with a deck that has four Aces missing, the player is at a disadvantage of 2.42 per cent, under best play. It may seem that the removal of the four Aces should affect matters much more than the removal of any other four cards, since Aces play such a unique role in the game. They are essential for a natural and for soft hands, and they make the most favorable pair. Wherever they appear, they seem to help the player. Thus some players may suppose that fluctuations in the proportion of Aces in the deck would have a much greater effect on things than fluctuations in the proportion of any of the other cards and that we ought simply to study Aces alone. However, we will see that Aces alone are not overwhelmingly important.

The computer was now asked to compute the player's advantage or disadvantage, using the best strategy, when playing with decks from which were removed in turn four Twos, four Threes, etc. The results for these and some other special decks are listed in Table 4.1. The corresponding best strategies were computed but have been omitted to save space.

Table 4.1 suggests that a shortage of cards having values 2 through 8 might give the player an advantage, while a relative excess of such cards might hurt the player. Conversely, a shortage of Nines, Tens, and Aces ought to hurt the player, while an excess of them should help him. A variety of winning strategies may be based on counting one or more types of cards. A good, simple winning strategy is based on counting the Fives. It will be described in detail in the rest of this chapter. The readers who find the basic strategy in Chapter 3 difficult should plan to adopt the Five-count strategy as their first winning approach to the game.

On the other hand, readers who learned the basic

strategy promptly should plan to use the point-count strategy of the next chapter as their first winning approach to the game. It offers many advantages over the Five-count strategy with only a moderate increase in the level of difficulty. These readers probably should not spend a great deal of time practicing the Five-count strategy. However, since the various discussions in the remainder of this chapter are important to the later strategies, it should still be thoroughly read and understood by those who are going on to the more powerful strategies.

A First Winning Strategy: Counting Fives

Table 4.1 shows that when four cards of one kind are removed from the deck, the greatest shift in the relative advantages of player and house is caused by removing the four Fives from the deck. The effect is even greater than when the four Aces are removed. More important, removing the Fives gives an advantage of 3.6 per cent to the player.

Now, suppose that the depleted deck contains no Fives but does contain enough cards for the next round of play, and that therefore no Fives will appear during the next round. It can be shown that these situations may be considered as mathematically identical with those that arise when hands are dealt from a deck which is complete except that the four Fives have been removed. Without attempting to give the detailed explanation for this, we simply point out that this means that if the player knows that no Fives can appear on the next round of play, and if he then follows what we shall call the "Five-count" strategy, on that round of play he will enjoy the 3.6 per cent advantage that is given in Table 4.1.

The Five-count strategy is given in Table 4.2. The format is that of Table 3.5.

Observe that the Five-count strategy is very similar to the basic full-deck strategy, which eases the burden on one's memory. In particular, note that the soft standing numbers are the same, that all the basic doubling-down situations also call for doubling down when the Fives are gone, and that the same statement is true for pair splitting except that a pair of Sixes is not split against a dealer's up card of Seven.

TABLE 4.1. *Player's Advantage or Disadvantage for Certain Special Decks.*

Description of deck	Advantage (in per cent) with best strategy
complete	0.13
Q(1)=0	−2.42
Q(2)=0	1.75
Q(3)=0	2.14
Q(4)=0	2.64
Q(5)=0	3.58
Q(6)=0	2.40
Q(7)=0	2.05
Q(8)=0	0.43
Q(9)=0	−0.41
Q(10)=0	1.62
½ deck	0.85 [0.93]
two decks	−0.25
four decks	−0.41
5000 decks	−0.58
Q(10)=4	−2.14*
Q(10)=8	−3.13
Q(10)=12	−1.85
Q(10)=20	1.89 [2.22]
Q(10)=24	3.51 [4.24]
Q(10)=28	5.06* [6.10*]
Q(10)=32	6.48* [7.75*]
Q(10)=36	7.66 [9.11]
Q(9)=Q(10)=0	9.92*
Q(8)=Q(9)=Q(10)=0	19.98*
Q(5)= . . . =Q(10)=0	78.14

Key: $Q(X) = Y$ means that a particular deck was altered by changing only the quantity Q of cards that have numerical value X so that there are now Y such cards. For example, $Q(2) = 3$ would mean that in the deck there are only three Twos instead of the usual four. "Two decks" means the cards are dealt from two ordinary 52-card decks that have been mixed together as one. The advantage with insurance is 0.12 per cent greater for $Q(2) = 0$ to $Q(9) = 0$. The player insures only if neither of his hole cards is Ten. For $Q(10) \geq 20$ the advantage with insurance follows in square brackets. Always insure when $Q(10) \geq 20$.

* Approximate.

TABLE 4.2. The Best Strategy When It Is Only Known That No Fives Can Appear on the Next Round of Play.*

Pair Splitting

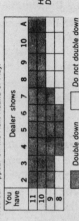

■ Split   □ Do not split

Soft Doubling

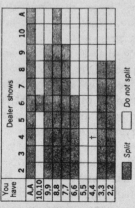

■ Double down   □ Do not double down

Hard Doubling

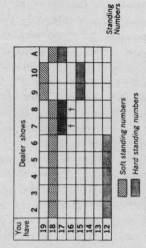

■ Double down   □ Do not double down

Standing Numbers

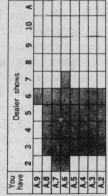

▨ Soft standing numbers   ■ Hard standing numbers

† Holding hard 16, draw if you hold two cards, namely (10,6) or (9,7), and stand if you hold three or more cards, for example, (6,4,4,2).

*The row (5,5) in the pair strategy and all columns headed by (a dealer's up card of) Five are meaningless, as no Fives can occur. These fictional squares have been included so that the format is identical with that of Table 3.5. We have shaded the table this way so it will be easier to memorize.

† Split only when doubling down on 8 is not permitted.

As a matter of fact, when all the Fives are gone it is perfectly acceptable to use only the changes in the hard standing numbers and otherwise play according to the basic strategy. The errors thus introduced primarily involve neglecting to split pairs or double down in several instances. Their effect is quite small. The player's advantage is decreased from 3.6 to 3.4 per cent. I suggest this to decrease the load on your memory. We shall adopt this "simplified Fives strategy" in all our calculations and discussions of the Fives method.

We now outline a simple method for winning at casino blackjack. Begin by making "small" bets and using the standard strategy. Watch the cards that are played and keep track of the Fives. When you see that all four of them have been used, check to see that the next round of play will come entirely from the remainder of the deck, and thus that no Fives will appear.

Now, you must place your bet before any of the cards are dealt in this next round. However, you know that you have better than a 3 per cent advantage on whatever you bet. Therefore, place a bet that is "large" in comparison to the ones you have been placing. When the cards are dealt, employ the simplified Fives strategy.

We have been recommending that if the Fives are used up before a certain round is dealt, the player should make a large bet and use the simplified Fives strategy. Now, it may happen that some Fives remain when a round of play begins and that all of them appear during that round. At the instant this happens the player should change to the simplified Fives strategy. For example, suppose he is dealt hard 7 and the dealer shows a Two. Suppose that when the player draws he receives the last remaining Five. He now has hard 12. The basic strategy says to draw. However, the Fives strategy now applies, and according to it he should stand.

This is to be considered a refinement and is not essential for winning with the Fives strategy. It improves the player's chances of winning some of his small bets, namely, some of those placed at the beginning of the round on which the last Fives appeared.

Suppose that you continue over many deals to place large bets when $Q(5) = 0$, and small bets otherwise. In those situations in which you made large bets, you win in the long run at a rate of above 3 per cent. With your small bets, you lose at a rate of about -0.2 per cent.* If the large bets are big enough compared to the small bets and if the favorable situations occur often enough, the profits from the big bets should both offset the losses from the small bets and leave a comfortable overall profit.

There are several questions that we must now answer in detail in order to make our instructions complete.

(1) How can you tell whether the remaining cards will be adequate for the next round of play?

(2) How often do favorable situations arise?

(3) How much larger than the small bets should the large bets be?

(4) How fast will you make money?

(5) How much risk is there?

(6) How much capital is required to start?

We will take these up in the order listed.

Counting the Cards

The check as to whether the remaining cards are adequate can be made in several ways. The surest way is to actually count how many cards have been used in play.

* One might wonder why, in the Fives strategy, the small bets do not instead win at the rate of 0.10 per cent, the average win rate using the basic strategy. The reason is that small bets are no longer made when the Fives are absent. Thus some favorable situations are removed from the small-bet realm and the remaining small-bet situations are, overall, slightly less favorable than average. The figure -0.2 per cent is inexact. The figure ranges from -0.2 to about zero per cent, depending on the number of players at the table. We selected a single number to simplify discussion. We made it pessimistic.

For example, after each round, you might say to yourself something like "Eleven cards have been played, and I have seen one Five." Count every card that is used as "played" but only count the Fives that you have seen. For example, if a card is burned, be sure to count it whether or not you see what it is. It is not necessary that you see every card that is used in play. If, however, you miss seeing any of the played cards, some of them may be Fives, in which case you will miss some favorable situations. For example, suppose after a certain round you see that seventeen cards have been played and that three Fives have been used. Suppose also that a Five has been burned and that you do not know this. Then, as far as you know, one Five may yet appear, so you will make a small bet and miss the opportunity of exploiting a favorable situation.

If your dealer habitually conceals the burned card, you may wish to request that he show it to you. It is sometimes difficult to know whether to make this request. It should not be made if you think that it will arouse the casino's suspicions that you are playing one of our winning strategies, for they may take countermeasures that are more costly to you than not seeing the burned card.

If the casino does not use the last card, incorporate this into your count from the beginning. The reason for this is that the particular count, when subtracted from 52, is supposed to give the number of cards yet to be played. Table 4.3 is a rough guide as to when the remaining cards will fail to be adequate for the next round.

Counting the used cards has other advantages besides telling the player whether the unused cards are adequate for the next round. First, the training in card counting is preparation for the more powerful, and also more difficult winning systems to be presented in succeeding chapters. Second, the count is an invaluable asset in the detection of cheating because a common device is to remove one or more cards from the deck. (One might wonder at this point

TABLE 4.3.

When the Deck Probably Will Be Adequate for a Full Round of Play, According to the Count of Used Cards

Number of players	Remaining cards usually adequate if count of used cards is no more than:
1	45
2	41
3	38
4	34
5	31
6	27
7	24

whether casinos have also tried adding cards to the deck. When two or more decks are being used, this can be done easily. I have only seen it done once when one deck was in use. That was risky. Imagine the shock and fury of a player who picks up his hand and sees that, not only are both his cards Fives, but they are also both Spades!)

Another well-known method of cheating which can often be detected by a card counter is called the "turnover." Though the name is apt, the experience is not a dessert treat. In the weak form of the turnover, the dealer watches to see whether the first half of the deck seems to favor the house strongly. If it does not, he continues normally, hoping that the latter half will. However, if the deck does favor the house during the first half, he secretly turns the deck over so that the used cards are on top and are replayed during the second half. In the strong form of the turnover, the dealer stacks the used cards from the first half of the deck as he picks them up after play. When the deck is about half-used, he turns it over and deals out stacked hands!

The unwary player generally does not remember which cards he has just seen. However, if the used portion contains a number other than 26 cards, the total deck will seem, to one who counts cards, to contain twice the number in the used portion instead of 52 cards. Further, even if the used portion contains 26 cards, the fraud may be detected unless it also contains two Fives. For the number of Fives in the total deck also seems to be, to one who is counting them, twice the number in the used portion.

For readers who do not want to count the used cards, there is a less satisfactory method for determining about how many cards remain to be played. It can be used if the dealer checks to see how near the end of the deck he is. He does this by pushing the lower cards slightly forward so that the upper edges of all the cards show slightly. Then the used cards, which are face up, appear "whiter" than the unused cards—provided that the unused cards, which are face down, do not have borders that make their edges white also. The relative thickness of the two portions makes it easy to estimate the number of unused cards remaining.

If you have a deck without borders, place a portion of the deck face up underneath the remainder. Then skew the deck by pushing the bottom cards forward slightly. There should be a clear line of demarcation between the two portions. From this you can estimate the amounts in each portion. With a little practice you can become quite skillful. If you attempt the same thing with a deck having borders it is harder, since the clear line of demarcation usually does not appear.

Here is a warm-up experiment that can be done with any deck; it should convince you that estimating the number of cards in a portion of the deck is not so difficult. First, square the deck by striking its edge against a smooth table top. Now try to break the deck into two equal portions. If necessary, transfer cards from one portion to the other until they appear equal. *Do not* place the two stacks side by side on the table top and match their height. That would destroy the purpose of this experiment, which is to introduce you to estimating by eye alone. After a few attempts you will find that rarely, if ever, are you "off" more than two cards.

Many people soon learn to divide the deck into two precisely equal parts almost every time.

An Improvement in the Fives Method

Suppose you keep track not only of the number of Fives remaining but also of the total number of remaining unseen cards. Then you can estimate whether or not the deck is Five-rich or Five-poor. One way is to divide the number U of unseen cards by the number F of unseen Fives. Normally $U/F = 13$. When U/F is greater than 13 the deck is Five-poor. (In the extreme case where $F = 0$, that is, when the deck has no Fives, U/F doesn't make sense. But you already know what to do then.)

The larger U/F, the larger your edge. When U/F is 26, for example, the edge is about 1.9 per cent (halfway from 0.13 per cent to 3.58 per cent. You should bet 2 or 3 units.

When U/F is less than 13, the deck is Five-rich. The casino has the advantage and you should make small bets.

The advantage of using U/F is that you find and exploit many additional favorable situations. The method works without change against any number of decks.

Frequency of Favorable Situations

The rate at which money is won depends upon how often favorable situations arise and is influenced by how many players are at the table. This dependence is shown in Table 4.4.

It clearly strengthens the player's advantage, when he is using the Fives strategy, to play in games in which there are no more than five players.

Variations in Bet Size

The instinctive answer to the question "How much larger than the small bets should the large bet be?" is "As large as possible," for it is the large favorable bets that are responsible for the profit. However there are some circumstances that need to be considered.

TABLE 4.4. *Variation in the Number of Known Favorable Situations, When Fives Only Are Counted, as a Function of the Number of Players.*

Number of players	Approximate number of times Fives are gone per hundred hands	Average amount in large units, won per hundred hands
1	9.8	0.33
2	5.9	0.20
3	6.5	0.22
4	3.5	0.12
5	6.0	0.20
6	0.9	0.03
7	1.7	0.06

If a player goes along steadily betting $1 and then suddenly, every once in a while bets $500, he may soon be the object of study by the casino operators. If he is winning, they are very likely to take countermeasures. One simple and effective method is to shuffle the deck after the player has made his large bet and before any cards are dealt. Although the player can then remove his large bet, his favorable situation is destroyed.

Thus it seems judicious to reduce the size of the bet variation to a level that does not attract so much attention. The first edition of *Beat the Dealer* has made the casinos very cautious. Consequently the large bets should be no more than three or four times the size of the smaller bets. Let us run through a simple calculation to see how costly this is.

Suppose we are playing 100 hands per hour head on with the dealer. Then, according to Table 4.4, there are about 9.8 favorable situations at 3.4 per cent in favor of the player and about 90.2 unfavorable ones at 0.2 per cent in favor of the house. If we are betting $1 and $500, we lose 0.002 × 90 × $1, or 18¢, on the unfavorable situations and gain 0.034 × 10 × $500, or $170, on the favorable situations, for a net profit of $169.82. If instead we bet $125 in the unfavorable situations, we would lose 0.002 × 90 × $125 or $22.50 in these instances but would again win $170 in the favorable situations for a net profit of $147.50.

It should be emphasized that these profit figures are rough average amounts for a very large number of hands. In any brief series of a few hundred hands, there will very likely be considerable deviations from these figures.

We can now use these figures to estimate the average hourly wage for the Fives system. Suppose that we are playing head on at the rate of 100 hands per hour. We saw previously that we average about $140 per hour when our bets range from $125 to $500. Therefore we should make $5.60 per hour when we bet from $5 to $20. The player who only bets from 50¢ to $2 will make a modest 56¢ per hour.

One skilled player whom I know asserts that he can play 350 hands per hour when playing head on. Betting from $1 to $500, he would average $170 × 3.5 or about $595 per hour. It is in the system player's best interest to be able to play rapidly. When more players are present, the fraction of hands that are favorable dwindles. Furthermore, since it takes longer to play out a round, each player gets fewer hands per hour.

Capital Required, Extent of Risk, Rate of Profit

We will now answer the questions:

How much capital is required to start?

How much risk is there?

What is the average rate of profit?

First you must decide how much your initial capital will be. You must NEVER, NEVER play with money that it will hurt you to lose. Besides the usual arguments against this, there is one more: playing with money that you cannot afford to lose produces psychological disintegration, bad play, and consequently a greater chance of defeat. Conversely, playing with money that means little to you leads to cool confidence and devastatingly accurate play.

Now you have cut your stake to a sensible level. Next you must decide how small to make the chance of ever losing your entire stake. For any stake, the player has many choices. If he plays boldly, taking a large chance of being ruined, he can make a comparatively large amount per hour. Instead the player may divide his stake into so many units that there is virtually no chance to lose it all. But the price paid for this is a considerable reduction in average profit.

As an indication of what to expect, suppose that small bets are 1 "unit," where a "unit" is an amount determined by you, the player. Suppose that big bets are 3 "units." Then with a stake of 150 units, the chances are less than 1 in 10 that you will ever lose your stake. They are more than 9 in 10 that your capital will grow indefinitely. If your stake is only 75 units, the chances are about 3 in 10 of eventually losing it and 7 in 10 of its continuing to grow as long as you care to play on.

Before we get on with learning practical winning strategies, we take time out in the next chapter to describe the original casino test of the first of these strategies, the now famous Ten-count method.

5

My Ideas Are Tested
in Nevada

I thought that the strategy based on counting Fives might make an interesting paper at an upcoming Annual Meeting of the American Mathematical Society in Washington, D.C. I planned to fly down from the Massachusetts Institute of Technology, where I was then teaching and where I made my blackjack computer calculations. A few days before the meeting, the society, as is customary, published abstracts of the two hundred or so talks that were to be given. Included was my abstract describing the Fives strategy, "Fortune's Formula: A Winning Strategy for Blackjack" [67].

Two evenings before I left for the meeting, I was surprised by a call from Dick Stewart, of the *Boston Globe* inquiring about the abstract. The paper sent a photographer out to take my picture; meanwhile I explained the basic ideas of my system to Mr. Stewart over the telephone.

The next morning I was amazed to see a picture of myself with a story on the front page of the *Boston Globe*

[4]. Within hours, the story and more pictures were released by the news services to their thousands of subscribing newspapers across the country [6, 27, 39, 43, 57, 78].

Following my paper in Washington, I was forced to give a press conference. After this I was televised by a major network and interviewed on a number of radio programs. When I returned to my office at the Massachusetts Institute of Technology, my desk was heaped with mail and phone messages, spurred by the continuing publicity [60, 65].

During the next weeks hundreds of letters and long distance phone calls rained in, the bulk of which were requests for copies of my paper and any further available information. Interspersed among this correspondence were a considerable number of offers to back me in a casino test of my system. The amounts proffered ranged from a few thousand dollars to as much as $100,000! Together they totalled a quarter of a million dollars.

Carefully, I screened the offers. I rejected an offer if the person or persons putting up the money could not prove that they could afford to lose their total investment. The reason is, of course, that there is some small risk of a very bad streak even with winning strategies, as we discussed earlier. I was also worried about the possibilities of being cheated.

Since the $100,000 was the most attractive, I considered it first. It was offered jointly by two New York multi-millionaires, whom I shall refer to as Mr. X and Mr. Y. They are both large-scale gamblers. Mr. Y once lost $100,-000 in one of the casino games without being seriously hurt financially. Mr. X's gambling activities involve hundreds of thousands and even millions of dollars in profits; he has been famous for years in gambling circles from Miami to Las Vegas. I later learned both that he was familiar with the exploits of "the little dark-haired guy" (Chapter 8) and that he had made large sums himself at blackjack. Thus he was thoroughly "sold" in advance.

Preparations

When I told Mr. X of my interest, he drove up from New York one Sunday. He showed me enough of his practical gambling knowledge and card skill to persuade me that he could quickly detect cheating. At the invitation and expense of Mr. X and Mr. Y, I flew from Boston to New York several times to discuss the system and to plan a trip to Nevada.

As the reader may have already learned from practice at home or in the casinos, the Fives system wins "too slowly" because the good situations that it locates are fairly rare. Fortunately I was already working on a far more powerful system when I announced the Fives system. This was the ten-count method, described in detail in Chapter 8. It was this method that I planned to use in the casino test. To make the story easier to follow, I describe this method briefly.

The player keeps track of two kinds of cards, Tens and non-Tens or "others." There are 16 Tens in each deck and 36 others. The player's edge is measured by the ratio of others to Tens. For one full deck, it is 36/16 or 2.25. When the ratio is below 2.25, the player has the edge. When it is above, the casino has the edge. Roughly speaking, the farther the ratio gets below or above 2.25, the greater is the effect.

The player has the edge half the time and his edge ranges up to 10 or 15 per cent. The casino edge only ranges up to about 3 per cent!

There were two main approaches that we could adopt for betting. One, which I shall term "wild," involves betting the casino limit whenever the advantage to the player exceeds some small figure, say 1 per cent. This method produces, on the average, the greatest gain in the shortest time. However in a short run of a few days the fluctuations in the player's total capital generally are violent, and a large bankroll is required. Mr. X and Mr. Y said that they would back this approach to the extent of $100,000 and that they would go farther if necessary.

The $10,000 Bankroll

I was not in favor of the wild approach since there were too many things I did not know about the gambling world. I also had no idea how I or my backers would react if I were to get behind, say, $50,000. Furthermore, the purpose of the trip from my point of view was to test my system rather than to make big money for Mr. X and Mr. Y. So I preferred being certain of a moderate win, rather than attempting a probable, but somewhat uncertain, big win. I therefore favored another approach, which I shall call "conservative" play. This involves betting twice the amount of the minimum bet when the advantage is 1 per cent, four times the minimum when the advantage is 2 per cent, and finally leveling off at ten times the minimum when the advantage is 5 per cent or more in the player's favor. I determined that if my bets would range from $50 to $500 (the highest casino maximum generally available), then $6,000 or $7,000 would probably be adequate capital. To be safe, we took along $10,000—a hundred one-hundred-dollar bills.

When the M. I. T. one-week spring recess came, Mr. X and I flew on a Thursday evening to Reno, where Mr. Y was to join us later. We checked into one of the large Reno hotels at about 2 A.M. and immediately went to sleep. Early the next morning we began investigating casinos.

The Warm-up

Our plan, insisted upon by me, was to proceed with caution. We would start "small," betting $1 to $10, and would gradually increase the amount of the bets as I gained experience. Eventually we planned to bet $50 to $500.

First we drove to a casino outside of town. In an hour or so of play I won a few dollars, and then when the establishment closed for three hours because of Good Friday, we returned to Reno. During the evening we investigated a number of casinos to determine which had rules that were most favorable. As the best spot for practicing, we selected a casino that dealt down to the last card and allowed the player to double down on any hand, split any pair, and insure. This is a more favorable set of rules than is ordinarily found.

After a sumptuous dinner and a rest, I returned alone to the casino we had chosen. It was then about 10 P.M. Mr. X did not accompany me because he is well known to that casino's owner and we did not wish to attract attention. I began by alternately playing for fifteen or twenty minutes at a time and then resting for a few minutes. Whenever I would sit down again I would always choose the table with the fewest players. My behavior pattern—I paused for thought and stared at all the cards played—made it apparent that I was using some "system." But system players are frequent, if not common, in the casinos. In fact, they are welcome as long as they are losing, and gradually I fell further behind until, by 5 A.M., I was down $100.

At this time, business fell off sharply and I was finally able to get a table completely to myself. My new dealer was particularly unfriendly. When I asked to be dealt two hands, she refused, saying that it was house policy that I must bet $2 per hand to play two hands. Since this change in the scale of betting would confuse my records of the evening's play, I refused. Besides, I was getting tired and irritable.

I pointed out to this dealer that at least eight other dealers had let me play two hands without complaint and therefore it could hardly be a house policy. She said that the reason was to keep other players from being crowded out. I remarked that there were no other players at my table, so her reason did not seem to apply. She became angry at this and dealt as rapidly as she could.

A few hands later, the ratio of others/Tens dropped to

2.0, a 1 per cent advantage for me. Being thoroughly annoyed by now, I broke my self-imposed discipline. I advanced to the $2 to $20 scale and bet $4. I won and the ratio advanced to 1.7, a 2 per cent advantage. I let my $8 ride and won again. The ratio obligingly dropped to 1.5, a 4 per cent advantage. I let my $16 ride and won again. I left $20 of this $32 on the table with the remark that it was time for me to take a small profit. The ratio fluctuated between 1.4 and 1.0 and I continued to make $20 bets. By the time we came to the end of the deck, I had recouped my $100 loss and had a few dollars' profit besides.

As I picked up my winnings and left, I noticed an odd mixture of anger and awe on the dealer's face. It was as though she had peeked for a brief moment through a familiar door into a familiar room and, maybe, she had glimpsed something strange and impossible.

This training session brought mixed blessings. I would regret my rash behavior in a few days, for the casino's operators took special notice of me. On the other hand, my attention was drawn to the doubling-up betting pattern that I had used in the last few minutes; it consisted of betting 1 unit, winning and letting the 2 units ride, winning and letting the 4 units ride, etc. This pattern of play resembles the well-known doubling-up system, or Small Martingale, which is widely used in almost every gambling game. The pattern I used above is not sensible for those gambling games in which the house has the advantage; but in blackjack, with the player's use of counting methods, it is as profitable as any other way of putting down money *at favorable times.* Furthermore, since the system is so widely and so unsuccessfully practiced, it makes an excellent disguise for the counting player. Also, the casual touch of leaving your chips untouched between hands seems nice.

A Hundred Here, a Thousand There

Sandy-eyed and stiff, I woke up early Saturday afternoon and had an elaborate breakfast. Afterward, Mr. X and I again visited the casino outside town. Within minutes, by playing the $10 to $100 scale, I won $200 or $300. Mr. X joined me and we played for a couple of hours. We accumulated $650, and the house began to shuffle the deck several cards before the end. Since the favorable situations arise with greatest frequency at the end of the deck, shuffling up can sharply reduce the rate of profit. Because we were only practicing, it seemed discreet for us to leave now and hope that we could come back later for a few full-scale hours.

Mr. X and I were still expecting Mr. Y in Reno. On Saturday evening Mr. Y arrived. After dinner Mr. Y and I set out to seek our fortune. We first visited the famous Harold's Club, an enormous building in the center of downtown Reno. We began to play at the $500-maximum tables. (The maximum generally ranges from $100 to $500 in Nevada, varying from casino to casino and frequently from table to table within a given casino. With our capital, we preferred the highest maximum possible.) In fifteen minutes we won $500, warming up at a $25 to $250 scale. Our dealer decided to alert the management of the casino. She pressed a concealed button with her foot. Within minutes Harold Smith Sr. and Jr. arrived. They exchanged pleasantries and politenesses with us, but they made their point: the deck would be shuffled as often as necessary to prevent us from winning.*

Most casino owners had learned, over the last decade, that some players would wait until very special combinations of cards arose, near the end of the deck, and that then they would sharply up their bet, sometimes going from $1 to $500. These players were stopped by shuffling the deck five or ten cards from the end.

Therefore, to be safe Harold Smith, Sr., instructed our dealer to shuffle no later than 12 to 15 cards from the end.

* Two years later, when Harold Smith, Jr., and I both appeared on Susskind's "Open End," young Smith scoffed, "System players? Why we send a cab to pick them up." I'm still waiting for that cab.

Fortunately for them, they waited to see the results. We were not planning any ulterior moves; we continued to use the same Tens strategy that we had used all evening. This strategy locates favorable situations after the first hand has been played, even if only four cards have been dealt.

A few minor yet favorable situations appeared and were exploited by us. Thereupon the deck was shuffled 25 cards from the end. Some favorable situations still arose. Finally the dealer began shuffling 42 cards from the end, that is, after only two hands had been played! This fencing went on for twenty minutes or so, and in that time a combination of bad luck, the club's unfavorable rules, and the shuffling allowed us to squeeze out only an additional $80. It seemed useless to continue playing at this casino, so we stopped.

We then visited a casino in one of the large hotels. We had been told that they used a "cheat" dealer on "big-money" players. After being cheated on the very first hand, in an incident described in detail in the chapter on cheating, we moved on.

Nine Hundred Dollars Bet on a Single Hand

In the next casino the maximum was only $300, but this limit was compensated for by excellent rules: the player could insure, split any pair, and double down on any set of cards. We purchased $2,000 in chips from the cashier and selected a table at which there were no other players. I lost steadily, and at the end of four hours of play I was almost $1,700 behind. I was quite discouraged. However I followed the pattern of countless hapless players before me (with, I hope, better reason) and decided to wait for the deck to become favorable "just once more" so I could recoup some of my losses.

In a few minutes the deck obliged, suddenly producing a ratio of others/Tens of 1.4, a 5 per cent advantage, which called for the maximum bet of $300. Curiously, my remaining chips amounted to precisely $300. As I tried to decide whether to quit if I lost this one, I picked up my hand and found a pair of Eights. They had to be split. I flung three $100 bills from my wallet onto the second Eight. On one of the Eights I was dealt a Three. I had to double down so I flung three more $100 bills onto this hand. There was, now $900 lying on the table—the largest bet I had yet made.

The dealer was showing a Six up and turned out to have a Ten under. He promptly busted. Now I was only $800 down. This deck continued to be favorable and the next went favorable after the first hand. In a few minutes I wiped out all my losses and went ahead $255. With this burst of good fortune, Mr. Y and I decided to quit for the evening.

Again the Tens system had shown a feature that would appear repeatedly: moderately heavy losing streaks, mixed with "lucky streaks" of the most dazzling brilliance.

The next afternoon Mr. X, Mr. Y, and I visited the casino outside town again. Before sitting down to play, I made a phone call. When I came back my friends told me the casino had barred us from play but that it would be only too happy to pick up our meal tab. I called over the floor manager and asked him what this was all about. He explained, in a very friendly and courteous manner, that the staff had seen me playing the day before and that they were very puzzled by my steady winning at a rate that was large for my bet sizes. He said also that they could not figure out what was going on but that they had finally decided, in the light of their previous experience, that a card-counting system was involved. My technique was becoming hard to detect.

Evidently they were discouraged when they estimated the power of the system that faced them, for the floor manager said that the owner had deliberated at length before deciding to bar us. The casino, he said, had fearlessly played against all card counters—and he reeled off a series of names that meant nothing to me—and had beaten them all, with one exception. He described the only player that had been previously barred as "a little dark-haired guy from Southern California." We have already mentioned this individual and will say more about him and other famous early players later on.

We returned to our hotel, and while my friends took care of business for a couple of hours, I passed the time away by betting $5 to $50 at the blackjack tables. Despite the annoying presence of a shill, I won about $550. At this point, the pit boss asked me to stop playing at the hotel and to tell the same to Messrs. X and Y and any other friends I might have. He did say, however, that we could enjoy unlimited drinks on the house. Immediately I had a Moscow mule and then went to tell my friends that they had been banned from this casino without their ever having played there.

It was almost suppertime Sunday when the three of us revisited the casino at which I had made the $900 bet. I was warmly remembered as the rich playboy of the night before who had been down $1,700 before wriggling off the hook by some quirk of fate. We were invited to dine, courtesy of the house, as a prelude to the evening's gaming festivities. After two $4 entrees of baked oysters on the half shell and various supporting dishes, capped with wine, I set out somewhat unsteadily for the gaming tables: I was truly a lamb readied for the slaughter. Within a few minutes, however, I was at peak alertness. After four hours of betting $25 to $300, I was ahead $2,000. Since I was beginning to tire, with the utmost reluctance I decided to return to my hotel.

I remember that casino fondly: the courtesy and hospitality, the spacious, attractive modern dining room with its fine cuisine, and the casino with its juicy little clusters of blackjack tables, the favorable rules, and last but not least, the free money.*

---

* This casino had its revenge. Nine months later I revisited it. A skillful cheat separated me from $600 in ten minutes (at $25 per hand) before I realized "times had changed."

The Twenty-Five-Dollar Minimum Game

My friends and I were again ready for action (action both in the customary sense and in the mathematical sense of the sum total of all bets made) early Monday afternoon. We drove to the south end (Stateline) of Lake Tahoe. About 6 P.M. we arrived at Harrah's large, brightly lighted gambling factory. It was jammed. I was barely able to get a seat at the blackjack tables.

A few minutes after I placed on the table the $2,000 worth of chips I had purchased from the cashier, a pit boss rushed over to invite me to dinner and the show. I in turn requested (with success) that my two friends be included. I began a game and within a few minutes—as I began to win—Mr. X joined me. In forty minutes, I won $1,300 and Mr. X, who was betting wildly, won $2,000. Then we took time out for our free dinner, which featured filet mignon and champagne. Within hours, destiny would present us with a bill for our "free" dinner. The charge? Eleven *thousand* dollars!

After dinner we strolled across to Harvey's Wagon Wheel. There were both the $500 limit and acceptable rules. As usual, I purchased $2,000 in chips from the cashier and selected the least busy table. From the beginning I was plagued by $1 bettors who came and went, generally slowing down the game, who concealed cards so that they were hard to count, and who created many other small annoyances.

Whenever a small bettor arrived at the table I pointedly reduced my minimum bet from $50 to $1. After a few minutes the pit boss "got the message" and asked me if I would like a private table. When I said it would "transport me with ecstasy," he explained that, in general, the club did not like the psychological effect of a private table on the other customers. However, with a trace of a smile, he said that a $25-minimum game could be arranged, and wondered if

that would be satisfactory. I promptly agreed, and a sign to
that effect was installed, which cleared the table of all customers but me. A small crowd gathered quietly to watch
their somewhat plumpish fellow lamb go to the slaughter.

Seventeen Thousand Dollars in Two Hours

After I had won a few hundred dollars, the pit boss
was amazed and delighted to see another "well-heeled"
lamb wander up and sit down at my table; it was none other
than my friend Mr. X, who thereupon "jumped in" the
game. I then took the responsibility, for both of us, for keeping the count and calling the signals. Within thirty minutes
we had emptied the table's money tray—the blackjack version of "breaking the bank." The once smiling pit boss trem-
bled with fear.

Other employees began to panic. One of our dealers
bleated to her boyfriend higher-up, "Oh, help me. Please.
Help me." The pit boss was trying to explain away our win
to a nervous knot of subordinates. While the money tray
was being restocked, the crowd swelled. They began to
cheer on their David again the casino Goliath.

One bystander blurted out rather loudly that he had
seen us off to a roaring start in Reno two nights earlier and
wondered if we had done there what we were now doing
here. As the pit boss listened attentively, we quickly hushed
up the bystander with tales of woe.

In two hours we broke the bank again. The great heaps
of chips in front of us included more than $17,000 in profits.
I had won about $6,000 and Mr. X, betting wildly, had won
$11,000. I was tiring rapidly. The aftereffects of our huge
dinner, the increased effort in managing two hands, and the
strain of the last few days were telling. I began to find it
very difficult to count properly and saw that Mr. X was
equally far gone. I insisted that we quit, and I cashed in
my $6,000. As I did so, I was startled to find three or four
pretty girls wandering back and forth across my path smiling affectionately.

After wending my Ulyssian way back to the tables, I watched, horror-stricken. Mr. X, having refused to stop playing, was pouring back thousands. In the forty-five minutes that it took to persuade him to leave, it cost the two of us about $11,000 of our $17,000. Even so, when we returned to our hotel that evening we were ahead $13,000 so far on the trip.

On Tuesday we paid a series of visits to a downtown club that had bad rules and shuffled five to ten cards from the end. We gradually but steadily lost about $2,000, playing $50 to $500. The player could double down on 10 and 11 only, could not insure, and the dealer hit soft 17. As will be seen in the chapter on rules variations, the player is whittled down at an average rate of slightly less than 1 per cent while awaiting favorable situations. Although these situations do arise, they are reduced somewhat in both frequency and favorability. Playing $50 to $500, the Tens strategy produces perhaps $500 per hour* with favorable rules and about $400 per hour with typical rules.† With the unfavorable rules just described, the strategy probably produces about $250 per hour, and the risk of bad fluctuations rises sharply.†

The new and powerful point-count strategy works quite well on these unfavorable casinos. That strategy, presented in Chapters 6 and 7, allows the player to count *all* the cards. It is no more difficult than the Tens strategy.

My friends and I recalled that the club in which I first practiced so lengthily had excellent rules and made a practice of dealing down to the last card in the deck. We decided to pay it a return visit. Mr. Y and I purchased $1,000 in chips and began to play. We immediately began to win, but within minutes the owner was on the scene. In a panic, he gave the dealer and the pit boss instructions.

Then an amazing performance began. Whenever I

* Assuming 100 hands per hour.
† These estimates are conservative. Records of tens of thousands of hands suggest that the true win rates are double these.

changed my bet size, the dealer shuffled. Whenever I varied
the number of hands I took (by this time I could play from
one to eight hands at one time and faster than the best
dealers could deal), the dealer shuffled. The dealer against
whom I had played last in my practice session was standing
in the background (had she "fingered" me?), saying over
and over in reverent tones how much I had advanced in
skill since the other night. Finally I happened to scratch my
nose and the dealer shuffled! Incredulous! I asked her
whether she would shuffle each time I scratched my nose.
She said she would. A few more scratches convinced me she
meant what she said. I asked whether any change in my
behavior pattern, no matter how minute, would cause her to
shuffle. She said it would.

I was now playing merely even with the house,* as the
shuffling destroyed nearly all my advantage (except that
gained from seeing the burned card). But by chance I
moved ahead about $300. I then asked for some larger-
denomination chips—$50 or $100—as all I had were twenties. The owner stepped forward and said that the house
would not sell them to us. He then had a new deck brought
in and carefully spread, first face down, then face up.
Curious, I asked why they spread them face down. Although
the practice is a common one in the casinos, seldom do they
examine the backs of the cards for a couple of minutes, as
these people were doing. The dealer explained that it was
believed that I had unusually acute vision (I wear glasses)
and could distinguish tiny blemishes on the backs of the
cards. This, they surmised, is what enabled me to foretell
what cards were going to be dealt. I scoffed, but the house,
still panicky as my wins continued, brought in four new
decks in five minutes.

* When the first edition of *Beat the Dealer* was written, I was under
the mistaken impression that shuffling up after every deal nullified my
system. So are the casino owners [31]. I have since realized that even
if the casinos shuffles after every deal, they can be beaten (see Chapter 9). The casino operators have some more nasty surprises in store
for them.

After disposing of that particular house theory, I pressed them to tell us what they thought about my "secret." The dealer claimed then that I could count every card as it was played, and that therefore I knew exactly which cards had not yet been played at each and every instant. Now, it is well known to students of mnemotechny (the science of memory training) that one can readily learn to memorize in proper order part or all of a deck of cards as it is dealt out. However, I am familiar enough with the method involved [14] to know that the information, when so memorized, cannot be used quickly enough for play in blackjack. So I challenged the dealer by rashly claiming that no one in the world could watch 35 cards dealt quickly off a pack and then tell me quickly how many of each kind of card remained.

She answered by claiming that the pit boss next to her could do just that. I told them I would pay $5 on the spot for a demonstration. They both looked down sheepishly and would not answer. I made my offer $50. They remained silent and ashamed. Then my friend Mr. Y increased the offer to $500. There was no response from these "sportsmen." We left in disgust.

At the next club that Mr. Y and I visited, the blackjack tables were packed, so we inquired about a private game. A balding, effeminate man scampered out and in nervous high tones told us that he knew what we were up to and they were on to us and "No, thank you." Another sportsman!

Since I had proved the system and the millionaires had business elsewhere, we agreed to terminate our little gambling experiment. In thirty man-hours of medium-and large-scale play, we had built $10,000 into $21,000. At no point did we have to go into our original capital more than $1,300 (plus expenses). Our experiment was a success, and my system performed in practice just as the theory on which it is based predicted it would.

Having an hour to kill before leaving for the airport,

we visited a friend of Mr. X at the Primadonna, a casino the friend operated. I was in favor of having a last big round of play, but Mr. X did not want his friend "hurt." Rapidly bored by the conversation, I wandered to the blackjack tables. I found three silver dollars in my pocket, inflicted on me as change by the last local merchant I had patronized. I decided to dispose of the silver dollars at the table. Soon a great sequence of favorable situations came along, and in five minutes my $3 became $35. Mr. X's friend never knew that a word from Mr. X had saved him more than $1,000 in that few minutes.

My trip to Nevada gives an ironic twist to the words of a casino operator who was being interviewed on a national television program. When he was asked whether the customers in Nevada ever walked away winners, he said, "When a lamb goes to the slaughter, the lamb *might* kill the butcher. But *we* always bet on the butcher."

The day of the lamb had come.

6

The Simple Point-Count System

Many readers of the first edition of *Beat the Dealer* were able to discover for themselves various "point-count" systems.* These systems were not presented in the first edition because the needed calculations had not been completed. The point-count systems will be valuable to both beginner and expert alike. They are especially useful in dealing with some of the more recent casino countermeasures against successful system players. This chapter presents a simple version of the point count. You will also hear the story of how one point-count player won $50,000 in the Puerto Rican casinos and single-handedly forced them to change their rules.

The Simple Point Count

When the deck is poor in high cards ($10, A$), Table 4.1 of Chapter 4 indicates that the casino has the advantage. When the deck is poor in low cards ($2,3,4,5,6$), Table 4.1

---

* It is permissible also to call ($2, 3, 4, 5, 6, 7$) low and ($9, 10, A$) high. The results are practically the same.

indicates that the player has the advantage.† This suggests a system in which the player somehow measures whether the deck has an excess of high cards (good) or low cards (bad), and bets accordingly. The simplest method is to count low cards $+1$ as they are seen, or "fall," and to count high cards -1 as they fall. Sevens, Eights, and Nines are not counted. Cards which are not seen are not counted. With one full deck and typical rules, the count starts at zero.

For example, if cards from a full deck are seen in the order $A,2,3,6,9,5,4,7$, the point values are $A(-1)$, $2(+1)$, $3(+1)$, $6(+1)$, $9(0)$, $5(+1)$, $4(+1)$, $7(0)$. The total number of points at any given time is the number we use. For example, with the cards in the order described above, the point *totals* are: before any cards are dealt, 0; after A, -1; after 2, 0; after 3 $+1$; after 6, $+2$; after 9, $+2$; after 5, $+3$; after 4, $+4$; after 7, $+4$.

To play the simple point count, all you do is keep track of the total points seen. Play your cards using the basic strategy. If the point-count total is zero or minus when you make your bet, bet only 1 unit. If it is plus, bet as many units as the point-count total.

In the example above, if it were time to bet just after you had seen the 6, you should have bet 2 units. If you

† A more recent example of someone's perhaps discovering a point-count system for himself is given in the *San Francisco Chronicle* of June 14, 1965. A feature story "Card Secrets for Sale" tells of a man who is said to have become interested in blackjack "purely by chance in March of 1964." By a curious coincidence, the *Life* story that internationally publicized *Beat the Dealer* appeared in March of 1964 [49]. The man offered his system for sale to San Franciscans for $1,000. He said each card in the deck is assigned one of four values: —10, —5, 5, or 10 (of course, in theory, —2, —1, 1, or 2 would have served as well). The assignment of such point values (one of several possible sets, but the others give practically the same results) can readily be derived from Table 4.1. It is: A is —10; 5 is 10; 2, 3, 4, 6, and 7 are 5; 8 is 0 (or 5, but 0 is better); 9 and 10 are —5. This system and the point count of this chapter, as well as innumerable other point-count systems, are all simplifications of the "ultimate" strategy that was presented in the first edition. That strategy made still finer gradations in point values for the cards, using the information in Table 4.1.

had just seen the 5, you should have bet 3 units. If you had just seen the 4 or the 7, you should have bet 4 units. Otherwise you should have bet 1 unit.

Notice that when all four Fives are gone, the point-count total is (on the average) + 4. The point-count calls for a 4-unit bet in these situations. So the point count and the Fives system agree that it is good to have all the Fives out. The advantage of the point count is that it finds many more favorable situations than the Fives system, and it finds them earlier. You win several times as fast.

You should now stop reading and take time out to practice the simple point count. If possible, have a friend deal to you. Play slowly enough so that you do not make mistakes. Do this even if you are ridiculously slow at first. As you practice, you will gradually speed up. Play with chips. This will add a touch of realism, and it will also give you an idea of how rapidly you will win. When you are playing the simple point count accurately and at a normal speed and feel quite comfortable with it, read on.

Refinements

After you are *completely comfortable* with the point count, there are several refinements which make it stronger.

If the point count is, say, + 5 and the deck is nearly complete, the deck is not as rich in high cards as it is if, for example, the point count is + 5 and only five cards are left. Then they are all high. So the advantage or disadvantage to the player depends not only on the point count but also on how many cards are left. If we take this into account we can play more precisely. The correct way to do this is to divide the point total by the number of *decks* left. The number we get is a still better one than the point total to use for betting purposes. For example, if the point count is + 1 and only ½ deck remains, we can bet $1 \div (½) = 1 \times (2/1) = 2$ units instead of only 1 unit. More important, this correction adjusts the point count for playing against casinos using 2 or more decks. In a two-deck game the point count for the almost complete two decks should be + 4 for a 2-unit bet, + 6 for a 3-unit bet, and so on. However, once the two decks have been played down to one deck, the betting should be the same as for one deck.

Later, in the advanced point count, or high-low, strategy (Chapter 7), we shall learn to keep a precise count of the remaining cards. This will allow us to compute our bets still more exactly.

It is also true that the strategy changes as the point count changes. As an extreme example, if only low cards are left, the player should always *draw* on hard 15.* Since he could draw at most a Six he could never bust, and drawing must improve his hand.

Roughly speaking, when the point count is plus, stand more often, double down more often, and split more often. When the point count is minus, draw more often, double down less often, and split less often. The details will be covered in Chapter 7. With this background on the strategy changes, I can describe my Puerto Rican adventure and "the Salmon's" great $50,000 win.

Henry Morgan and I visit Puerto Rico

After the first edition of *Beat the Dealer* was out, I appeared on "I've Got a Secret" (April, 1964). My "secret" was, of course, that I could rapidly and consistently win at casino blackjack under the usual playing conditions. But Gary Moore, moderator of the program, had a secret for the panelists too. His secret was that Henry Morgan was to try out the system in the Puerto Rican casinos on a bankroll of $200. Henry was to report back to the program the following week.

I decided to go down, too, and see what the Puerto Rican casinos were like. Messrs. M and N, two young New York entrepreneurs (also the promoters of an abortive

---

* To experts: I can think up one-in-a-million situations in which he shouldn't, but to give them here would only clutter up the discussion.

$25,000 challenge match with a well-known Las Vegas casino), bankrolled my play.

I spent an enjoyable afternoon with Henry Morgan in the New York offices of "I've Got a Secret," attempting to teach him the point count. But his jokes were so much more interesting, and he himself so uninterested in the dry routine of "training," that I settled for showing him the main parts of the basic strategy. Hopefully, he would manage to break even. (Profits would go to charity, of course.)

I stayed with Messrs. M and N in the luxurious La Concha hotel. It is one of about ten in San Juan that have casinos. Henry settled elsewhere. Casino hours were generally from 8 P.M. to 4 A.M. N and I arrived about midnight, got settled, and played for a couple of hours to get the feel of things. M had come in several days earlier and had won about $1,000 so far. He showed us around, and it soon became apparent that there were significant differences between the Puerto Rican game and the Nevada game.

First, the Puerto Rican casinos were government regulated. This meant that official printed rules of the game of blackjack were posted on the wall of each casino, in plain sight. The same was true of many procedures. The casinos couldn't suddenly change the rules on me, as they had in Nevada. You may recall, for example, that in the test of the Ten-count system (Chapter 5) Harold's Club shuffled up on me and another club refused to sell me large-size chips. The two other games that were generally played, roulette and craps, also had their rules and regulations posted. The rules for the games were uniform (a few options were allowed) for the several casinos we visited.

As an added protection for both customer and casino, a government man was on duty in the casino playing area at all times. And every reasonable effort was made to inform the patrons of these facts. This contrasts with the situation in Nevada.

The blackjack game itself was dealt face up from two

decks. The cards were dealt from a dealing box, or "shoe." This makes the sleight-of-hand card trickery so often encountered in Nevada (but so seldom noticed; see Chapter 10 for details) much less likely. Don't think you can't be cheated from a dealing box. You can, as we'll see shortly. But the variety of cheating methods are fewer and the chances of catching them are higher. So they definitely discourage cheating.

To further discourage cheating, two decks with different color backs (e.g., one red deck, one blue deck) were generally used. The top of the dealing box was mostly open and you could see the color of the back of the top card. If you watched closely you could sometimes also see the color of the back of the card dealt to you. The dealer's hand often covered the card so well during the instant before the card was turned face up that the color couldn't be determined. If you saw a red card and got a blue one, you would know you were cheated.

Another nice feature of the Puerto Rican casinos is that no liquor is served in them. A favorite device of the Nevada casinos is to ply their customers with "free" liquor. This is often done deliberately, to impair the player's judgment and to remove his inhibitions. It works. I have seen well-heeled drunks who pay their employees one dollar an hour fling thousands across a blackjack table in a few minutes. And I have seen poor drunks write checks they couldn't cover. The last are perhaps the saddest cases. The Puerto Rican casinos willingly serve unlimited snacks—sandwiches, Cokes, etc. The atmosphere is quiet and relaxed. Evening dress is the rule.

The blackjack rules allowed the player to play as many initial hands (before pair splitting) as there were empty places. There were seven places, so a player alone could play seven hands at a time. The greater the number of hands per hour, the greater the profit from the system used, so we generally played this way—alone with up to seven hands.

The rules were like the typical rules of Chapter 2, with one important exception. Doubling down was restricted to totals of hard 11 only. When questioned, the casinos said that soft 21 could also be counted as 11 and doubled down on (the printed rules seemed to imply it also). They were quite amused by the question and wondered what fools would ever double down on soft 21.

Here's an example where doubling down on soft 21 is the best play! Suppose you are keeping track of total points, total remaining cards, and total remaining Aces. Suppose you have just been dealt (*A,10*) and the dealer shows a *10*. Suppose also that the point total is now + 3, there are three cards left, and no Aces left. Then the three cards left unseen are all Tens. So the dealer's hole card is a Ten. He has 20, he can't draw, and you will win one and a half times your original bet from your natural, or blackjack, if you stop now. But if you double down, you will get another 10 for a total of ordinary 21. Your 21 beats the dealer's 20 and you walk away with twice your original bet, instead of only one and a half times it.

Admittedly this is an expert play. You would not be expected to do it after learning only the simple point count. However, once you have mastered Chapter 7, there is a good chance you will be capable of such feats. The point of the story here is that precision play of this sort was beyond the imagination of the casino personnel we met.

There was one other important rule in Puerto Rico. The betting limits were $1 to $50, compared with $1 to $500 in most of the larger Nevada establishments. The maximum win rate in Puerto Rico would only be about one tenth what it was in Nevada. So M's win of $1,000 in three or four days would correspond to a win in Nevada (multiplying all bets by 10) of $10,000.

After the evening's warm-up we turned in about 5 A.M. One of the great strains of these little ventures is readjusting the body's schedule to the reversed hours that gamblers tend to keep.

Enter the Salmon

Before we arrived, M had noticed a system player who was having great success, playing every night and winning steadily. He and M became acquainted.

The casino personnel nicknamed him the Salmon (pronounced Sal-*moan*, with the stress on the second syllable). Inspired by the first edition of *Beat the Dealer*, he had begun to play about six months earlier, with a stake of $200. I said in the book that this stake would give the player a 99 per cent chance to go on winning indefinitely. There was only a 1 per cent chance that an extreme run of bad luck would ever wipe out the stake plus accumulated winnings.

The Salmon took me at my word and got to work. He found that the Ten-count was too laborious, so he discovered for himself the simple point count plus refinements. When we met him, his original $200 had grown to $20,000.

The Salmon put on a splendid and effective show. He would come into a casino, spot an empty table, and purchase several thousand dollars' worth of chips, which he stacked in several great irregular columns, up to a foot or two in height. The columns of chips looked like monstrous superkings in checkers. He scattered his great columns of chips all over the layout, like pieces in a game. But he always managed to scatter them so that they effectively blocked anyone else from playing. While he played, the Salmon kept up a disarming and amusing line of patter with the nearby casino personnel.

The evening after I arrived, recent copies of *Life* magazine [49] reached Puerto Rico. In them was a twelve-page story, with pictures, about me and *Beat the Dealer*. The book had also moved onto the *New York Times* non-fiction best-seller list. I was then recognized by the casino personnel. After the casinos shut down at 4 A.M., M, N, and I had a snack with some of the people from one of the casinos.

We learned that the Salmon had been winning regularly for several months, but no one knew the true extent of his winnings.

I asked why he was called the Salmon and was told that it was because he was like a fish that swam up stream. "But we'll get him in the end," a casino boss said. "We call it *a la larga* [in the long run]," he said. "And we call it 'in the long run,' " I said. Salmon later told me that "Salmon" was Puerto Rican slang for "jerk."

The casino view that the Salmon was a jerk was further reinforced by the way he played some of his hands. At the end of the deck, in apparent recklessness or disgust, he would sometimes hit a blackjack again and again until it busted. Likewise with a pair of Tens or a pair of Aces. Other times he would stand on a pair of deuces! Surely this was madness, the casino personnel would say to me again and again.

I could only smile and say that it certainly was difficult (for them, that is) to understand how such playing could lead to anything but disaster. I pointed out that my basic strategy, the Fives strategy, and the Tens strategy, all forbid such plays. Was Salmon mad? Far from it.

The Salmon was using "end play," as described in the first edition (see also Chapter 8). Let's start with an example. The Puerto Rican casinos dealt two decks all the way to the end. The last card of the two decks was pulled back, unplayed, however. Suppose now that the simple point count is, say, −8 and there are (roughly) about 16 cards left to be played. Recall now that the Salmon has blocked off the table with great stacks of chips. Since there are seven places, he can play from one to seven hands on each deal. He now takes, say, four hands and bets $1 on each hand (remember, the deck is *bad*). He and the dealer between them get ten cards on the deal. Suppose that the Salmon's first hand is $(10,10)$, his second hand is $(A,10)$ and the rest are small cards. He hits the $(10,10)$ until it busts. Then he does the same with the $(A,10)$ if possible. Then he draws to the small-card hands, without busting any of them. When the deck is exhausted, the used cards are reshuffled. The $(10,10)$ and $(A,10)$ cards are in this reshuffled group. The table is covered with small cards which are not.

The next deal comes from a shoe which is poor in low cards. The Salmon bets $50 per hand and has the advantage. On the average he will have the advantage down to the end of the two decks. At that time end play is again used to exert control over the composition of the next shoe.

The Salmon deliberately lost some $1 bets so he could win some $50 bets. And the operators decided that he was a jerk.

We promptly adopted the Salmon's tactics. And for several evenings the casinos would see one, two, and sometimes three master players march up to the empty tables just after opening time. The "masters" would cover the tables with great irregular towers of chips and then begin to play one to seven hands at a time. The Puerto Rican dealers were very fast (on the average much faster than the Las Vegas dealers, in my opinion). Yet each of us could play still faster than the fastest dealer while we were supposedly counting myriad cards and mentally computing at a great rate.

At the end of a shoe one evening, I had been losing for an hour or so. My dealer had a ten up. I had seven hands with various totals. I was using the variation of the point count where $2,3,4,5,6,7$ are $+1$, 8 is 0, and $9,10,A$ are -1, when they fall. The deck had run out on the deal, and the point count was zero. Therefore the one unseen card, which was the dealer's hole card, was a "zero." So the dealer had an Eight in the hole for a total of 18.

As the play of the hands developed after the reshuffle, I had to hit several totals of hard 17. They all busted.

The dealer looked up scornfully, saying to me with a

laugh, "So you count the cards, amigo. Why (ha, ha), I'll bet you even know what I've got under here." A couple of the other dealers grinned. So I said, "Why, you have an Eight under there." The dealer laughingly summoned several of the other dealers and the pit boss. He explained contemptuously that the Americano "expert" said that he had an Eight in the hole. A babble of uncomplimentary remarks in Spanish passed back and forth.

I was tired and about ready for a break. I had made an occasional counting error over the last hour.* There was a chance I would be wrong (better for me if I was, probably). Then the dealer turned over his hole card. It was an Eight. And the babble in Spanish raged anew.

We played on for five nights. During this time our capital fluctuated rather violently, considering the small bet size. At one time we were a couple of thousand dollars behind. This made us redouble our playing efforts. During these few days I was playing at my peak. I would count Aces, points, and remaining cards, or Aces, Tens, and non-Tens, and sometimes not just three but four or five quantities. I was making perhaps one or two counting errors an evening! Yet I was having difficulty pulling ahead.

I looked for cheating and found only one incident. M and I were playing at the same table in one of the crowded clubs (*not* La Concha). Our dealer seemed extraordinarily clumsy. Two cards kept trying to come through the slit in the side of the dealing box. They would jam and he would fumble around. We finally got tired of this and moved to another table. Then that box was moved to our table! We moved again and the box moved again! M asked to examine the dealing box, and we summoned the government man. Nothing appeared to be wrong.

But we knew shoes that deal seconds have been made.

---

* It is an important and interesting fact that errors in card counting, if they are "random," i.e., have no intrinsic "patterns" or "tendencies," do comparatively little harm to a system player!

They were commonly used, for example, in faro as played
in the old West. A clever mechanism was concealed in the
thin side panels. If this were such a shoe, one of the side
panels might be hollowed out. There was one long side
panel and two shorter end panels. We tapped both end
panels with a chip. They sounded the same. Then we tapped
the longer panel. It gave a higher tone. By the laws of
physics the tone should have been lower. We tested other
apparently identical dealing boxes. Their long side panels
gave out the expected lower tone. Conclusion: we would
avoid this club from now on.

Why didn't we ask that this box be confiscated and the
matter be investigated? Mainly because we were unable to
communicate with this government man. He didn't seem to
understand English and he didn't seem to know what we
were driving at. Of course, any effective action would have
to be initiated there, on the spot, with the evidence at hand.
Once it disappeared, so did the chance of making an effective complaint.

We ended our stay with a joint win of a little under
$2,000, which barely covered the cost of a luxurious vaca-
tion for four. This would correspond to a win of almost
$20,000 in Nevada with its higher betting limits. But we
should have won much more. Playing conditions were ideal,
and dealing down to the last card enabled us to use end
play very strongly. Also, in the same amount of time the
Salmon piled up $7,000 with play that was not as strong
as ours. We found very little difference between our winnings when we used a point count and when we used a Ten
count.

An Interesting Idea for End Play

Finally, the day before we left, I realized how we could
make a fortune in Puerto Rico as long as they dealt down
to the end of the deck. My idea had begun to form a couple
of evenings earlier. M was very impressed with the courteous, friendly, relaxed atmosphere in the Puerto Rican

casinos. It was so different from his experiences in Las Vegas and the other Nevada gambling meccas. He asked N to count Aces for him with chips. This worked fine. Next it was Tens and Aces. This worked too. Finally, N would take turns fully relieving us of our counting chores by assisting with the chips. Surprisingly, what N was doing appeared to pass unnoticed.

This made me realize that it was feasible to count *all* the cards so that, every so often, we could know the dealer's precise hole card. The profits could be spectacular. We practiced with a miniature tally sheet in our rooms the next afternoon. My idea was that the player could be assisted by a helper who counted all the cards with a tally sheet. We would start at the beginning of two fresh decks by taking seven hands at $1 each and playing them out with the basic strategy. This would be repeated, to use up most of the two decks quickly. Now, 102 cards are actually played out of the 104 cards in two decks, since the top one is burned and the bottom one is pulled back. About three cards are used per hand. So in a round of seven hands plus the dealer's, about 24 cards are used. In three such rounds, about 72 cards are used, leaving about 30.

Suppose that this in fact happens in an actual game. We would next take some number of hands that *guarantee* that the box will run out in the following round. But it must run out after the dealer gets his hole card so we can then tell from our count what that hole card is.

We take enough hands so there will be 16 or a little fewer cards left after the round. The reason for the uncertainty at this stage is that we can't control in advance how many cards, if any, the dealer will draw. In this case, five player hands plus two cards drawn or six player hands plus no cards drawn would use up 12 cards. Since the dealer's hand uses up 2 more cards of the original 30, this would leave 16 cards less the number the dealer draws to his hole card.

Suppose it turns out that he draws two cards. Then

there will be fourteen cards left to play on the final deal of the box (plus one card that will not be played). We now take six hands and bet the maximum of $50 on each of them. The fourteen cards are just enough to deal out all our hole cards and the dealer's two cards. Our cards are face up, we can see all of them, as well as the dealer's up card. We now try to hit the first hand, no matter what its value. The dealer pulls out the last card, notices that it is the last card, and refuses to give it to us. Once we have seen and counted this card, the only card left unseen is the dealer's hole card, and we now know from our count what that card is.

After the dealer shuffles the used cards, we get on with playing out our six hands. He asks us whether we still want to draw to our first hand. (If the casino rule is that we had to draw to this hand because we had requested a card *before* the shuffle, we would have countered by only betting $1 on this hand.)

Playing Strategy When the Dealer's Hole Card Is Known

We play this hand and the five others with a new "basic" strategy. The term "basic" means again that (for simplicity only) we are not considering information about any cards other than the dealer's two cards and the hole cards of the hand being played.

Instead of a separate playing strategy for each dealer's up card, we now have a separate strategy for each pair of dealer's cards. There are fifty-five such pairs. The strategies were calculated in detail by Julian Braun and forwarded to me some months before the Puerto Rican trip. The results are given in Table 6.1.

Note that the strategies are very much alike against dealer's cards of the same hard total.

Braun calculated that the player's advantage in a one-deck game with typical rules, when he knows the dealer's hole card, is 9.9 per cent. (Just as a matter of general inter-

est, Braun found that if the dealer also won all ties in such
a game, the player would still have an edge of 2.1 per cent
We omit the somewhat different player strategy for this
situation.)

Value of Knowing the Dealer's Hole Card

We could have averaged $25 ($50 per hand × 5 hands
× 10%) or so per box by using the complete count of all
the cards to determine the dealer's hole card. We played
at least six boxes an hour. At six hours per evening (rest
two) this would have been $900 per evening—a "living
wage"! But we were unable to become proficient enough,
as a team, to get started before we left. And the Puerto
Rican rules were changed soon afterwards, as a result of
the Salmon's exploits, so we never had the opportunity to
take advantage of the method.*

In an ordinary game the player sometimes finds out
what the dealer's hole card is. The first time this happened
to me was at one of the big strip hotels in Las Vegas. One
man was playing alone at a $5-minimum table. He was
betting $200 to $500 on each hand and winning rapidly.
What's more, he and the dealer seemed to be getting along
just fine. I sat down and bet $25 to $100, figuring that my
activities would go unnoticed alongside his bigger bets.

I soon noticed that when the dealer had 17 or more,
the player always hit hands of 16 or less. Once when the
dealer had a *10* up and a *6* in the hole, the player stood on
12! Then I noticed that the dealer was tipping off the
player as to whether he had a "stiff" (12-16) or a probable
stiff (4-6), by looking unnecessarily long at his hand. If
he had a pat hand (17-21) or a probable good hand (7-11

---

* There was little chance in any case that I personally could have
won much money in Puerto Rico. The intense public interest and
publicity which surrounded me at the time made the casinos acutely
aware of my activities. As soon as my winnings became impressive, the
rules would have been changed. The Salmon's success depended on the
fact that he concealed the true extent of his winnings for a long time.
When he "opened up," the casinos did change the rules, as we shall see.

TABLE 6.1. *Basic Strategy When the Dealer Exposes His Hole Card.*

| Dealer's Hand Hard | | | | | Dealer's Hand Soft | | | | |
Dealer Shows	MH MS	Double-Downs Hard	Soft	Splits	Dealer Shows	MH MS	Double-Downs Hard	Soft	Splits
2,2	14 18	10,11		1,7,8	A,A	16 18	11		1,8
2,3	13 18	10,11		1-3,6-9	A,2	15 18	10,11		1,7,8
2,4	12 18	9-11	17,18	1-3,6-9	A,3	14 18	10,11		1,7,8
3,3	12 18	8-11	13-19	1-4,6-9	A,4	13 18	10,11		1,2,6-9
2,5	17 18	10,11		1-3,7,8	A,5	13 18	9-11	17,18	1-3,6-9
3,4	17 18	9-11		1-3,7,8	A,6	17 18			1-3,6-8
2,6	17 18	10,11		1,7-9	A,7	18 19			2,3,7-9
3,5 or 4,4	17 18	10,11		1-3,7-9	A,8	19 19			9
2,7 or 3,6	17 19	10,11		1,8,9	A,9	20 20			
4,5	16 19	10,11		1,8,9					
2,8	16 19	11		1,8					
3,7 or 5,5	16 19	11		1					
4,6	17 19	11		1					
2,9	16 18			1					
3,8	15 18			1					
4,7	14 18			1					
5,6	14 19			1					
2,10 or 3,9 or 4,8	12 18	8-11	13-19	1-4,6-9					
5,7 or 6,6	12 18	8-11	13-20	1-4,6-10					
13 total	12 18	7-11	13-20	1-4,6-10					
14-16 total	12 18	5-11	13-20	1-4,6-10					
17 total	17 18			2,3,6-8					
8,10	18 19			2,3,7-9					
9,9	18 19			3,6-9					
9,10	19 19			9					
10,10	20 20								

MH=Minimum hard standing total
MS=Minimum soft standing total

The player's advantage in this game is 9.9 per cent. (It is assumed that the game is played in the normal way except that the dealer exposes his hole card.)

or soft 12 to soft 16), he looked at his hand only for an instant. He was telling the player what to do. Play for 17 (or more) if he looked only briefly at his card. Stand on hard 12 if he looked a long time.

Of course, the details only became apparent after a while. But I caught onto the "stiff" or "pat" part right away. In the next twenty minutes the player won an additional $2,000. He tipped the dealer $300. I won about $500 in the same time. Then the dealer went off duty and the situation broke up.

When a dealer in Nevada has an Ace or a Ten up, he checks his hole card before giving additional cards to any of the players. If he has a natural, the hand is settled then and there. If the dealer is inexperienced, he may give away some information about his hole card. For example, if the up card is an Ace, and the hole card is small, some inexperienced dealers see very quickly (from the lack of "paint") that it is not a Ten, and pause only briefly. If the up card is a Ten, the reverse happens; now they wonder if they have an Ace. If the hole card is large, they can see this very quickly. If it is small, they must bend the hole card up quite a lot before deciding it is not an Ace. Mr. F (see Chapter 12) gave me this tip in gratitude, after I had won $1,600 by standard methods for him and Mr. X at the Las Vegas Club in a couple of hours one evening. Mr. F and his cronies call this dealer giveaway the "tell."

A La Larga: The Salmon Wins $50,000

We left Puerto Rico with fond memories, hoping to return on another pleasure trip after school was out in the summer. The Salmon was fearful that our visit and impending return would speed the day when the Puerto Rican goose would stop laying golden eggs for him. He began to bet the limit in all favorable situations. Within another two months his winnings rose to $50,000.

The Salmon had played an average of five or six nights a week, seven or eight hours a night, for nine months. Figuring forty hours a week for forty weeks, that's 1,600 hours. At 150 hands an hour, he played 240,000 hands. And he won $50,000 without ever making a bet over $50 per hand (except in the comparatively few instances when he doubled down). This is the longest casino test of the point count that I know of. It is a spectacular demonstration of our methods in action.

In Las Vegas, with a $500 limit (and an honest game!) the result would have been $500,000 instead! Despite the "modest" amount that he won, the Salmon's win is one of the great marathon feats of gambling history. *A la larga*—the long run—showed the Puerto Rican casinos the handwriting on the wall.

The Rules Are "Changed" in Puerto Rico

The casinos then stopped their practice of dealing to the end of the box. Against good players (the Salmon, M, and N, for example) they reshuffled as often as was necessary.

I learned the sad news when the Salmon called me to see what could be done against this. I advised him to hunt for greener pastures. Try Panama, Curacao, Aruba, and (cautiously) the Grand Bahamas. Stay out of Haiti and the Dominican Republic: it may take the U. S. Marines to get your winnings (if any) out. I told him that Las Vegas was a harsh, pitiless place. At that time there was a particularly severe cheating problem. But he could win heavily there if he could dodge the cheating, or if he adopted the "paper-route" technique described in Chapter 9. He tried Las Vegas and was soon stripped of $2,500.

The last I heard from the Salmon was that he was waxing prosperous in balmy Puerto Rico. He was the proud owner of a fleet of taxicabs which paid him $100 a week each in rentals. He dallies on the beautiful warm beaches and in the night clubs, living the life of a playboy. Every once in a while he hears of a "good" blackjack game in the Caribbean and rushes over to "kill" it. But he longs wistfully for the good old days when money grew on trees, and all he had to do was go out and pick it.

7

The Complete
Point-Count System

Like the simple point count, the complete point count, or
high-low system, had occurred independently to many readers of *Beat the Dealer*. However, it was first announced to
the scientific public by Harvey Dubner, then of Simmons
Precision Products Corporation in Tarrytown, N.Y. Dubner
presented his results at a panel session of the 1963 Fall
Joint Computer Conference, a national semiannual meeting of thousands of computer experts. This time the conference was in Las Vegas, Nevada. The panel session was
on the use of computers to study games of skill and chance.

The leading experts in the field talked of their work
in analyzing such games as blackjack, baccarat, roulette,
and go. Besides Dubner, the panelists were: Julian Braun
of the IBM Corporation (Braun's detailed blackjack calculations, based on his extensions and refinements of my
original computer program, are the most accurate in existence, and he has kindly allowed them to be used through-

out this revised edition); Richard E. Sprague, director of computer systems, Touche, Ross, Bailey and Smart (author of *Electronic Business Systems*); William E. Walden, then of the Los Alamos Scientific Laboratory and now director of the Computing Center at the University of Omaha (he and I jointly developed a system for Nevada baccarat, and our winnings forced the casinos to remove certain formerly profitable bets from the layout); and Allan N. Wilson (author of *The Casino Gambler's Guide*, a recent coverage of the principal casino games; readers of this book will be interested in comparing Wilson's lengthy coverage of blackjack). Theoretical remarks were made by Robert E. Kalaba, a mathematician from the RAND Corporation and an expert on gambling systems like the Kelly system (see p. 23).

I was the moderator of this panel session.

An enthusiastic Dubner made great claims for the complete point-count method. His calculations supported his claims. And his play in the casinos (for low stakes) during the computer conference was very successful. The interest of the other experts was aroused. Braun then made detailed calculations. (His computer techniques were based on the methods developed and used to work out the Ten-count strategy for the first edition.) Although these showed that there were some inaccuracies in the details of Dubner's results, Braun found that the complete point count was a powerful and effective winning blackjack strategy.

Exactly how much better or worse it is than the Ten-count method is not known. But they are of comparable power. In an era of casino countermeasures, tightening rules, and dealers who are finally learning to count cards, the complete point count is a welcome new weapon. The beginner should probably read through to the Ten-count chapter and then choose either the complete point count or the Ten-count as the first powerful winning strategy to be mastered. For those who are already proficient in the Ten count, the complete point count is a valuable alternate strategy and should also be learned, if possible.

Counting the Cards

In the complete point count, we simply perfect the refinements of the simple point count. The first step is to have an exact count, rather than a rough idea, of the number of unplayed cards. So we will need to remember *two* numbers, total points, as before, and also total unseen cards. The count of total unseen cards is quite simple. For one deck, start your count at 52. Each time you *see* one of the cards used in play, subtract 1 from the current total. If a card is played and you do not see it for one reason or another, *do not* change your total of unseen cards. Adjust the total if you see the burned card or if the dealer flashes the bottom card.

When we were only counting total points, the cards could be counted any time during or after the play of the hand. The only important thing was to have the total point count available in time to decide how much to bet on the next deal. You could even wait until a hand was over and then count the cards all at once. We can still do this when we are counting both total unseen cards and total points, provided we use the information merely to arrive at the proper bet size. We still play our hands with the basic strategy.

When we want to use our card-count information to vary the strategy for playing the hands—to improve on the basic strategy—we can still count this way. But it will be still better to adjust the count as soon as we see a card, without waiting. This method of counting is called the "running count." It is something like a full-court press in basketball: your count totals are always ready. You don't let up, except when the cards are completely reshuffled, or the dealers change, or you change games.

Naturally the running count is more tiring. If counting

is easy for you, use it; it is best. If counting is hard for you, don't worry. Figure out the easiest way to count and use that. Your results will be almost as good. Perhaps they will even be better because you will be less likely to make mistakes.

Here is how we use the new count to decide on the bet size. Divide the point total by the total of unseen cards. For example, in one-deck game, if 5,5,3,8 fell, the point total would be +3, 48 cards remain (unseen), so we get 3/48 or about 0.06. I find that the easiest thing to do is to estimate the nearest per cent. In this case it would be 6 (per cent), because to change to per cent means to multiply by 100. I call this final number the high-low index.

If the same cards had been seen from *two* complete shuffled decks, we would have +3 points and 104−4 = 100 unseen cards and a high-low index of 3. If there were 4 decks to start with and *A, 10, 10, 9, 8, 8, 10, A, A* fell, the high-low index would be −6/199 or −3 (per cent).

The Bets

Bet 1 unit for a high-low index of 2 or less. For a high-low index of 4, bet 2 units. In general, bet half the index in favorable situations; index 6, bet 3; index 8, bet 4; index 10 (or more!) bet 5. For index values between these, you can shade your bets up or down, at your pleasure. For example, if the index is 5, you can make the bet corresponding to an index of either 4 or 6, that is, either 2 or 3 units. The reason for betting no more than 5 units, even when the index is over 10, is simply that the casinos get too excited if you do.

Drawing and Standing

The basic strategy is the best way to play against a complete deck. But if some cards are missing and we know something about them, we usually can improve on the basic strategy. As a simple (and unrealistic) example, suppose that the game is being dealt from four well-shuffled decks and that the only cards left are Fours or smaller. Then the player should *draw* on hard 17, no matter what the dealer's up card is. This is in sharp contrast to the basic strategy, which recommends standing on hard 12 against an up card of 4, 5, or 6.

FIGURE 7.1. Player's Advantage as High-Low Index Varies.

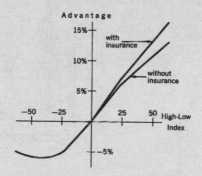

To use Table 7.1, you look in the square corresponding to the dealer's up card and your hard total. If it says "draw" or "stand," things are easy. Suppose instead that you find an index number. Then you stand if your index is greater than the one in the table. But if your index is less than or the same as the one in the square, you draw.

For example, suppose the dealer shows a Ten and you have hard 13. The table says draw, no matter what your index. Now suppose you get a *Three*. You now have hard 16. If your index is 02 or less, draw. If it is more than 02, stand. (Warning: Minus indexes are less than plus indexes. Using < for "less than," we have in general . . . < −3 < −02 < −01 < 00 < 01 < 02 . . . and so on. So a large index *with a minus* is *less than* a small index *with a minus*. This may be news to readers who are not used to negative numbers.)

TABLE 7.1. Using the High-Low Index to Draw or Stand with Hard Hands.

You have	\	\	\	Dealer shows	\	\	\	\	\
	2	3	4	5	6	7	8	9	10	A
18 or more	STAND									
17	STAND									-15
16	-21	-25	-30	-34	-35	10	11	06	00	14
15	-12	-17	-21	-26	-28	13	15	12	08	16
14	-05	-08	-13	-17	-17	20	38	DRAW	DRAW	DRAW
13	-02	-05	-09	-08	-01	DRAW	DRAW	DRAW	DRAW	DRAW
12	14	06	02	-01	00	DRAW	DRAW	DRAW	DRAW	DRAW

The indexes are in per cent. Stand if your index is larger than the appropriate entry in the table. Draw if your index is less than or equal to the appropriate entry in the table. The table assumes that you have already adjusted your index to account for the dealer's up card.

TABLE 7.2. Using the High-Low Index to Draw or Stand with Soft Hands.

You have	2	3	4	5	Dealer shows 6	7	8	9	10	A
19 or more	STAND									
18	STAND							29	12	-06
17	DRAW									

Draw if you have a soft total of 16 or less.

TABLE 7.3. Hard Doubling Down with the High-Low Index.

You have	2	3	4	5	Dealer shows 6	7	8	9	10	A
11	-23	-26	-29	-33	-35	-26	-17	-16	-10	-03
10	-15	-17	-21	-24	-26	-17	-12	04	14	
9	03	00	-05	-10	-12	05	05	22		
8				22	11	14	17			
7				45	21	14	17			
6					27	18	24			
5					20	26				

Double down if your index is greater than the index in the square. Do not double down if it is less than or equal to the index in the square. Do not double down if a square is blank or if it is not in the table. The table assumes you have already counted your hole cards and the dealer's up card.

TABLE 7.4. Soft Doubling Down with the High-Low Index.

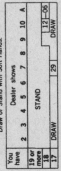

You have	2	3	Dealer shows 4	5	6
A,9		20	12	08	08
A,8		09	05	01	00
A,7		-02	-15	-18	-23
A,6	*	-06	-14	-28	-30
A,5		21	-06	-16	-32
A,4		19	-07	-16	-23
A,3		11	-03	-13	-19
A,2		10	02	-19	-13

Double down if your index is greater than the index in the table. Do not double down if it is less than or equal to the index in the square. Do not double down if a square is blank or if it is not on the table. The table assumes you have already counted your hole cards and the dealer's up card.

* Double down with (A,6) versus a 2 only when the index is between 01 and 10.

TABLE 7.5. Using the High-Low Index to Split Pairs.

Your pair	2	3	4	5	Dealer shows 6	7	8	9	10	A
A,A	▓	▓	▓	▓	▓	▓	▓	▓	▓	▓
10,10					-33	-24	-22	-20	-17	
9,9	25	-17	10	06	07	19	08	-16	-22	10
8,8	▓	▓	▓	▓	▓	▓	▓	▓	24*	-18
7,7	-22	-29	-35							
6,6	00	-03	-08	-13	-16	-08				
5,5										
4,4		18	08	00	05†					
3,3	-21	-34					06†			
2,2	-09	-15	-22	-30						

If a square is shaded, always split.
If a square is blank or omitted, never split.
If a square contains an index number, split if your index is higher. Do not split if your index is lower.

* Split (8,8) against 10 only if the index is below 24.
■ Split (4,4) against 6 when the index is greater than 05 only if doubling down is not permitted.
† Split (3,3) against 8 when the index is above 06 and also when the index is below -02.

Table 7.2 gives the drawing and standing strategy for soft hands. It is read in the same way as Table 7.1. Notice that the soft strategy is the same as in the basic strategy except for three cases.

1. With soft 17 against 7, and an index greater than 29, stand (the basic strategy says draw).

2. With soft 18 against *10*, and an index greater than 12, stand (the basic strategy says draw).

3. With soft 18 against an Ace, and an index of −06 or *less,* draw (the basic strategy says stand).

The first two exceptions are quite rare in actual play and may be neglected until you become an expert. Since −06 is fairly close to 00, we can simplify the third exception by saying: hit soft 18 against an Ace if the deck is moderately unfavorable. So the results of Table 7.2 can be simplified to: For drawing and standing with soft hands, play the basic strategy with just one exception. With soft 18 against an Ace, hit when the deck is moderately unfavorable.

Doubling Down

The doubling-down strategy for hard hands appears in Table 7.3. Note that doubling down with a total of hard 5 is sometimes best play! Such facts were undreamed of until only recently. Notice that the more favorable the deck, the more likely we are to double down. Double down if your index is larger than the table entry. Do not double down if your index is less than the table.

Table 7.4, which gives the strategy for soft doubling, is read in a similar way. Once again, the more favorable the deck, the more frequently we double down on soft totals (and the greater the profits).

Pair Splitting

Table 7.5 gives the strategy for pair splitting with the high-low index.

Insurance

If the index is greater than 08, insurance should be taken. Otherwise it should not be taken. A more detailed discussion of insurance will be found on pages 106–11.

Advantage and Frequency of Favorable Situations

Figure 7.1 illustrates how the player's advantage changes as the index changes. Notice the gain insurance produces. It is also interesting that the player gains more when the index is positive than he loses when it is negative. This is because the player can vary his strategy. Therefore he can to some extent reduce the disadvantage he gets from poor decks. He can also increase the advantage he gets from good decks.

The figure gives the impression that if the index is negative enough, the player regains the advantage. This impression is correct but the situations are rare in play. Table 4.1 shows some of these situations. For example, when Q(10) = 0, giving an index of −16/36, or −44 per cent, for an otherwise full deck, we have a player edge of 1.62 per cent. However, the average situation with an index of −44 is still disadvantageous for the player, as indicated in Figure 7.1. When the index is −100, in which case the remainder of the deck consists of cards having values of Two through Six only, the player always has an advantage, averaging something like 50 per cent, and depending on the precise cards remaining.

Table 7.6 gives an idea of how often various values of the index, and various advantages, arise in actual play. Notice that the chances of various negative values of the index exactly balance the chances of the corresponding positive values. To illustrate the use of the table, note for example that after five cards have been dealt, the index is between 05 and 15, 9.5 per cent of the time. It is between −5 and 05, 81 per cent of the time. It is between −15 and −05, 9.5 per cent of the time.

TABLE 7.6. *Advantage and Frequency of Favorable Situations.*
Table lists the percentage of the time that various situations arise.

	Advantage (per cent) with insurance												
	−5.7 above	−6.0 to −5.7	−6.0 to −5.9	−5.9 to −5.1	−5.1 to −3.5	−1.1 to −3.5	−1.1 to 1.4	1.4 to 4.3	4.3 to 7.2	7.2 to 9.7	9.7 to 12.7	12.7 to 14.6	14.6 above
	High-Low Index Ranges												
	below −55	−55 to −45	−45 to −35	−35 to −25	−25 to −15	−15 to −05	−05 to 05	05 to 15	15 to 25	25 to 35	35 to 45	45 to 55	above 55
Number of cards seen													
0							100.0						
5						5.5	81.0	9.5					
10					.4	15.8	67.6	15.8	.4				
15					2.7	27.5	39.5	27.5	2.7				
20				.5	6.8	24.2	37.0	24.2	6.8	.5			
25			.1	1.9	5.9	24.0	36.2	24.0	5.9	1.9	.1		
30		.1	.7	3.2	9.4	18.3	36.6	18.3	9.4	3.2	.7	.1	
35		.5	2.7	3.4	13.5	23.2	13.3	23.2	13.5	3.4	2.7	.5	
40	.7	1.3	2.6	5.0	19.3	13.8	14.6	13.8	19.3	5.0	2.6	1.3	.7
45	5.3	0	7.3	12.1	0	16.3	18.0	16.3	0	12.1	7.3	0	5.3

For convenience, this table was based on 200,000 random shuffles. A direct calculation could also have been made. Because of rounding off the 4th and 8th lines fail to add up to 100 per cent.

8

A Winning Strategy
Based on Counting Tens

The strategy to be discussed in this chapter, the "Ten-count" strategy, was the "workhorse" winning system introduced in the first edition. It is comparable in power to the complete point count. The expert should know both systems. The beginner should attempt to master only one at first. Readers who know the point count may either skip this chapter or read it through quickly.

The advantages this strategy finds for the player generally range from 1 to 10 per cent. The large advantages yield heavy winnings. The smaller advantages give the player camouflage: it is natural in this strategy, as with the point count methods, to vary the bet size with the advantage in small steps all the way from small waiting bets to a size several times these bets. This is less conspicuous than just two kinds of bets, "large" and "small."

Another camouflage advantage of the detailed Ten-count strategy is that the player's decisions greatly depend on the composition of the unused deck. Suppose for example that the dealer has an Ace up. Sometimes the player should hit hard 17; other times he should stand on hard 12!

One might wonder, in view of Table 4.1, how a strategy based on Tens could give greater advantages than one based on Fives. Card for card, Fives have more effect than Tens: four Tens added to the deck give the player an advantage of 1.89 per cent, whereas four Fives removed from the deck give an advantage of 3.58 per cent. The solution is that there are 16 Tens in the deck and only four Fives. Therefore much greater deviations from the average can occur in the number of Tens than in the number of Fives.

Effect on Player's Advantage as Proportion of Tens Varies

The richer the deck is in Tens, the better off the player is, generally. We shall now think of the deck as divided into two kinds of cards, "Tens" and "others." During play, we shall keep track of the number of others and the number of Tens that have not yet been seen. Thus, with the Tens strategy, we take into account only the cards we see, as we see them. From these two numbers we shall determine "Ten richness" by computing the ratio "others/tens" (others *to* tens). For example, suppose the complete deck is shuffled and prepared for play. For the complete deck, the "count" is 36 others and 16 Tens, or simply (36,16). The corresponding ratio is 36/16 or 2.25. The approximate advantages for several ratio values are given in Table 8.1 for quick reference.

Learning to Count

Our first goal will be to learn to keep count of the others and Tens yet to be played while also playing with the standard strategy. Here is an exercise which should be done as a preparation in learning to count. Take a shuffled complete deck, and turning cards over one at a time, "count"

TABLE 8.1 *Approximate Player Advantage in the Ten-Count Strategy.*

Others/Tens	Normal approximate advantage (in per cent)
3.00	−2.0
2.25	+0.1
2.00	1.0
1.75	2.0
1.63	3.0
1.50	4.0
1.35	5.0
1.25	6.0
1.16	7.0
1.08	8.0
1.00	9.0

them and drop them face up onto a discard pile. For example, I have just picked up the deck on my writing desk. I count, "(36,16); *3* of Spades (35,16); *5* of Clubs (34, 16); *3* of Hearts (33,16); *4* of Diamonds (32,16)—the ratio is now 2.00 and the hands dealt now give the player a 1 per cent advantage (Table 8.1); *3* of Diamonds (31, 16); *6* of Spades (30,16); Queen of Diamonds (30,15), etc." A few cards from the end of the deck, stop and record your count. Then see if the remaining cards agree with your count of them. In the example above, when I stopped, my count was (2,1) and the last three cards were the deuce of Clubs, the Nine of clubs, and the King of clubs, in agreement with the count.

The first few times it may take you two minutes or more to go through one deck without any mistakes. However, you should be able to drop your time, in six or eight fifteen-minute practice sessions, to between twenty-five and fifty seconds. Fifty seconds is more than adequate and twenty-five seconds is excellent. I had trouble getting below twenty-five seconds until I found that it takes me twenty to twenty-five seconds to turn over the cards whether I count them or not. For those who want to push this exercise to the limit, there is a way to break this twenty-five-second barrier. Remove a few unknown cards and spread the remaining cards face up in a row, with enough of each card showing so that it may easily be identified. Then count, by reading from left to right or from right to left. You should learn to be equally at ease reading in either direction. Your count should check against the unknown cards that were removed.

Shortly after I had practiced spreading the cards for rapid counting, there was an opportunity to use this skill. I was examining a certain casino to see if it cheated and began, naturally, by watching the table where the most money was being risked. After the shuffle, it was the casino's practice to have the dealer place a joker face up on the bottom of the deck to separate the used cards from the unused ones. At the end of one deal the joker had vanished! The amazed players asked to examine the deck. The dealer spread it in the standard fashion and then scooped it up again in about four seconds. Even with the rapid count I could only count the first 12 cards.

The players demanded a closer look at the deck. This time the dealer gave them ten or fifteen seconds. When I reached 38 cards (28,10), the dealer began to scoop them up again slowly. I quickly counted the number of cards remaining, without regard for denomination. There were 20 left: the deck had 58 cards! Of course, the dealer still had not allowed the players enough time to examine the deck. They called for a new deck and requested that the pit boss examine the old one. He counted the old deck off to one side, holding it in such a way that no one else could count along with him.

When he finished counting, an odd expression flickered across his face. Then, without offering a word of explanation to the players about the recent puzzling events, he left, taking the old deck with him. The trusting players continued the game and soon forgot the matter. The pit boss had accurately judged their naïveté.

While you are increasing your counting speed with this exercise, you should also practice maintaining a count while someone deals to you and you play the basic strategy. Have them deal slowly enough so that you can count easily. Play with chips and start with 200 units. Before each hand, use your count to estimate the ratio. Then vary your bets according to the scheme given in Table 8.2.

Roughly speaking, whenever the ratio is between 2 and

TABLE 8.2. *A Conservative Betting Scheme for the Ten-Count Strategy.*

Ratio	Bet (in units)
above 2.00	1 (minimum)
2.00-1.75	2
1.75-1.65	4
below 1.65	5

1.65, we are betting about twice as much, in units, as our advantage is in per cent. We level off below 1.65 at 5 units so the variations in our bet size will not unduly alarm the casino. You do not need to perform division in your head to figure out the ratio exactly. Rough guesses, say to within 0.1 or even 0.2, are very satisfactory.

Insurance

There is one important change from the standard strategy that you should take into account at once. Whenever the ratio is less than 2.00, take insurance if the opportunity (dealer's up card an Ace) presents itself. If the ratio is 2.00 or more, do not insure. This is reasonable. If the deck is Ten-rich and the dealer shows an Ace, he is more likely than usual to have blackjack. You are allowed to check your hole cards (and you may have been able to see other player's hole cards too) before insuring. You have also seen the dealer's up card. All this can be taken into account, if you wish, before deciding whether to insure.

We can calculate either the player or the house advantage from the insurance bet whenever we know the number of Tens and non-Tens. We illustrate this calculation for the case in which hands are being dealt from one complete deck, a situation which represents the average house advantage. In this instance, the dealer's up card is an Ace. Since the dealer's Ace is visible, there are 51 possibilities for his hole card (assuming at the moment, for simplicity, that we do not use our knowledge of our own two hole cards as well), 16 of which are Tens. On the average, the player wins twice the amount of his insurance wager 16 times out of 51, or 31.4 per cent of the time. The bet is lost 35 times out of 51. The average house edge is $35/51 - 2 \times 16/51$, which is $3/51$ or 5.9 per cent.

If you wish to take into account your hole cards, there are three cases to consider. If your hole cards are $(10,10)$, the house edge is $35/49 - 2 \times 14/49$, which is $7/49$ or 14.3 per cent. If they are $(10,x)$, where x represents a non-Ten, the house edge is $34/49 - 2 \times 15/49$, which is $4/49$ or 8.2 per cent. If you hold (X,X) the house edge is $33/49 - 2 \times 16/49$, which is only $1/49$, or 2.0 per cent.

Insurance was originally introduced by the casinos as just one more way of fleecing the player. It is ironic that a bet providing such an average advantage for the casino can be turned against the house. The trick, of course, is simply more of what we have been doing all along. The average house advantage is 5.9 per cent, but there are times when the advantage is in favor of the player. At these times we insure and otherwise we do not. For example, when the count before the deal is $(10,10)$ the player's average profit on an insurance bet is $2 \times 10/19 - 9/19$, which is $11/19$, a healthy 58 per cent of the amount of the insurance.

Once when I played in a large club in Reno, I noticed

that it had no insurance bet. Since one of the owners was standing at my elbow (for I had begun to win rapidly and they had rushed up to stop me), I asked why there was no insurance. He said that because it hurt the players, it was taken out for their benefit. As a large bettor (large bettors generally are humored and given little privileges), I asked that I be allowed to insure, explaining that it gave me a feeling of security when I made large bets (when the count was (10,10) for example!). My request was refused without an explanation. I later learned that one player, using end play (discussed later), the insurance rule, and card counting, had taken at least $40,000 from this casino before he was stopped.

Many dealers and players alike share two widespread misconceptions about the insurance bet. They often become annoyingly insistent in their attempts to "correct" a player who does not share their view. The first misconception is that a player should always take insurance if possible when dealt a natural. The argument is that if the dealer has a natural also, the hands themselves will tie but the insurance bet wins one unit. If the dealer has no natural, the player's natural wins 1.5 units and his insurance bet of 0.5 unit is lost. Again the win is 1.0 unit. In either case the player has a sure profit of one unit. Why not take it?

First, I will show you that there is a case in which the insurance bet is wasteful. Suppose that you are counting Tens and non-Tens, and that after you see your hole cards and before you decide whether or not to take insurance, you find that all Tens have been played. In this event the dealer cannot have a natural. If you insure your natural, you have a sure profit of exactly 1.0 unit, as discussed above. However, you know that your natural is a winner, so if you do not insure, you have a sure profit of 1.5 units. In this instance, to insure is to throw away 0.5 unit.

Now, suppose the deck had only one Ten and, say, eight non-Tens left. Should you insure? No, because even

TABLE 8.3. The Ten-Count Strategy, Based on The Value of the Ratio When a Running Count of the Cards Is Kept.

Hard Doubling

You have	Dealer shows									
	2	3	4	5	6	7	8	9	10	A
11	3.9	4.2	4.8	5.5	5.5	3.7	3.0	2.6	2.8	2.2
10	3.7	4.2	4.8	5.6	5.7	3.8	3.0	2.5	1.9	1.8
9	2.2	2.4	2.8	3.3	3.4	2.0	1.6			0.9
8	1.3	1.5	1.7	2.0	2.1	1.0				
7	0.9	1.1	1.2	1.4	1.4					
4,2		1.0	1.2	1.3						
3,2		1.0	1.1	1.1						

Standing Numbers

You have	Dealer shows									
	2	3	4	5	6	7	8	9	10	A
19										2.2*
18									3.1*	2.2
17										3.1
16	3.9	4.5	5.3	6.5	4.6		1.2	1.7	2.2	1.4
15	3.2	3.6	4.1	4.8	4.3			1.4	1.9	1.3
14	2.7	2.9	3.3	3.7	3.4			1.1	1.6	1.2
13	2.3	2.5	2.6	3.0	2.7				1.3	1.1
12	2.0	2.1	2.2	2.4	2.3				1.1	1.0

▨ Soft standing numbers ■ Hard standing numbers

*Against an Ace, the soft standing number is 19 if the ratio is above 2.2. It is 18 if the ratio is 2.2 or less. The hard standing number against an Ace is 18 when the ratio is above 3.1. It is 17 when the ratio is 3.1 or less.

Pair Splitting

You have	Dealer shows									
	2	3	4	5	6	7	8	9	10	A
A,A	4.0	4.1	4.5	4.9	5.0	3.8	3.3	3.1	2.2	2.6
10,10	1.4	1.5	1.7	1.9	1.8					
9,9	2.4	2.8	3.1	3.7	3.2	1.6		4.2		1.5
8,8									1.5*	4.8
7,7	2.4	2.6	3.0	3.6	4.1	3.4				
6,6										
5,5										
4,4	1.3	1.6	1.9	2.4	2.1†					
3,3						1.1*	2.4*	4.2*	5.3*	
2,2		3.1	3.8			1.1*			3.8*	

*Numbers followed by an (*) are read in reverse fashion. For example, split (8,8) against a 10 when the ratio is above 1.6 and not otherwise.

†Split (4,4) against a 6 when the ratio is 2.1 or less only if doubling down on 8 is not permitted.

Soft Doubling

You have	Dealer shows					
	2	3	4	5	6	7
A,9	1.3	1.3	1.5	1.6	1.6	
A,8	1.4	1.7	1.8	2.0	2.0	
A,7	2.0	2.2	3.3	3.8	3.5	
A,6	2.1	2.5	3.2	4.8	4.8	1.1
A,5	1.6	1.9	2.5	3.1	4.0	
A,4	1.6	1.9	2.4	3.0	3.2	
A,3	1.5	1.8	2.3	2.9	3.0	
A,2	1.5	1.7	2.1	2.6	2.7	

TABLE 8.4. A First Approximation to the Ten-Count Strategy.*

Pair Splitting

You have	2	3	4	5	6	7	8	9	10	A
A,A										
10,10	1.4	1.5	1.7	1.9	1.8					
9,9										1.5
8,8						1.6			1.6*	
7,7										1.4
6,6										
5,5										
4,4			1.3	1.6	1.9					
3,3							1.1*			
2,2							1.1*			

*Numbers followed by (*) are read in reverse fashion. For example, split (8,8) against a 10 when the ratio is above 1.6 and not otherwise.
†Split (4,4) against a 6 when the ratio is 2.1 or less only if doubling down on 8 is not permitted.

Hard Doubling

You have	2	3	4	5	6	7	8	9	10	A
11									1.9	1.8
10										0.9
9						2.0	1.6			
8	1.3	1.5	1.7	2.0	2.1	1.4	1.0			
7	0.9	1.1	1.2	1.4	1.4					
4,2			1.0	1.2	1.3					
3,2			1.0	1.1	1.1					

Soft Doubling

You have	2	3	4	5	6	7
A,9	1.3	1.3	1.5	1.6	1.6	
A,8	1.4	1.7	1.8	2.0	2.0	
A,7	2.0					1.1
A,6	2.1	1.1				
A,5		1.6	1.9			
A,4		1.6	1.9			
A,3		1.5	1.8			
A,2		1.5	1.7			

Standing Numbers

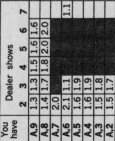
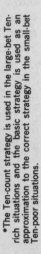

You have	2	3	4	5	6	7	8	9	10	A
19									2.2	2.4
18								1.7	1.9	1.3
17										
16							1.2	1.4	1.9	1.3
15								1.1	1.6	1.2
14									1.3	1.1
13									1.3	1.1
12			2.0	2.1					1.1	1.0

Legend:
- (hatched) Soft standing numbers
- (black) Hard standing numbers

*The Ten-count strategy is used in the large-bet Ten-rich situations and the basic strategy is used as an approximation to the correct strategy in the small-bet Ten-poor situations.

though your insurance bet may win, you are probably throwing it away. On the other hand, if all the remaining cards were Tens, the dealer would be certain to have a natural also, and insurance wins 1.0 unit for you. If in imagination we let the deck get richer and richer in Tens, there ought to be some critical point beyond which insurance is profitable and below which it is unprofitable. It is the same point we recommended above. When the ratio falls below 2.0, insure. When it is above 2.0, do not insure. When it is exactly 2.0, there is, in the long run, no gain or loss on the average, so you can do as you please. Actually, *in this one instance*, to insure a natural will reduce the fluctuations in your capital. Thus if you have limited capital there is a minor advantage in doing so for a ratio of exactly 2.0.

The same arguments apply, with greater force, to the second misconception, which is "Insure a good hand and do not insure a poor one."

Strategy Tables

There is a complication in giving the Ten-count strategy. For the best possible play, we must vary our strategy as the ratio varies. For each ratio there is a corresponding strategy. Fortunately, all these separate strategies can be combined into a single chart, given in Table 8.4 or, better, in Table 8.3. The player using Table 8.3 keeps a "running count"; that is, he keeps track of the cards as they appear. With his up-to-the-second information, he is able to play his hands with great precision. Many readers of the first edition became experts with Table 8.3 (Table 5.3 in that edition). Tables 8.3 and 8.4 have our usual format, with one exception: some of the squares, instead of simply being shaded, have numbers. In the case of doubling down and pair splitting, these numbers are to be interpreted as follows. If the ratio is equal to or less than the number in the square, consider the square shaded; that is, split the pair or double down. If the ratio exceeds the number in the square, consider the square blank; that is, do not split the pair or double down. There are two numbers marked with an asterisk (*). These numbers have an opposite interpretation. If the ratio is greater than such a number, consider the square shaded. Otherwise, consider it blank.

Referring to Table 8.3, read the minimum standing number chart as follows. The soft standing numbers are the same as for the basic strategy except when the dealer's up card is an Ace. In that case, it is 18 as usual for ratios of 2.2 or less. It is 19 for ratios above 2.2. The hard standing number against an Ace is 17, as usual, if the ratio is less than or equal to 3.1 (but greater than 1.4). For ratios above 3.1 it is 18. The hard standing number for up cards of 2 through 10 and for an Ace when the ratio is 1.4 or less, is read, as follows, from the chart. For a given ratio, shade all squares having numbers greater than or equal to that ratio. The lowest shaded square is the correct standing number. Alternately, one might think of all the squares with numbers greater than or equal to the current ratio as the goal. Draw until your total equals or exceeds the totals represented by these squares. For example, if the dealer shows a 4, the standing numbers are: 12 for ratios of 2.2 or less; 13 for ratios above 2.2 but less than or equal to 2.6; 14 for ratios above 2.6 but less than or equal to 3.3.

Notice that the hard standing numbers against cards 2 through 6 have all dropped to 12 by the time the ratio drops to 2.0, which is the point at which we begin increasing our bet size. You may recall that the hard standing numbers for cards 2 through 6 were also all equal to 12 for the Five-count strategy. As the ratio becomes larger, which corresponds to a shortage of Tens, these hard standing numbers rise. They reach 17 against a 2 when the ratio is above 3.9 and against a 3 when is above 5.0.

The most important part of this strategy to incorporate into your plan is the standing numbers chart. This gives you most of the theoretical advantage. However, if you wish to add other parts of the strategy, the order of importance is the same as in the standard strategy: first learn hard doubling, then pair splitting, and soft doubling last.

Memorizing Table 8.3 in its entirety seems like too much work. When I began play in the casinos with the Ten-count strategy, I only knew approximately the standing number and doubling down parts of Table 8.3. For soft doubling, I knew even less. I played the standard strategy until the ratio fell to 1.4 and then I doubled down on all soft totals from 13 to 20 against cards 2 through 6. Time and time again dealers have smiled as though I were insane when I doubled down on soft 20 and turned it into a poor total. But their smiles have disappeared when they bust themselves.

The running count sometimes yields gains at the end of the deck because the player can figure out from it what the dealer's hole card is. I played a hand in which this made a difference of $250. I had bet $125. I had glimpsed the other players' hole cards, and so when my turn came (I was the last to play), I knew two cards remained, both Tens. The dealer's hole card was therefore a Ten and only one card, a Ten, remained unplayed. If I were to draw, it would be offered, then the dealer would see it was the last card, and as was customary he would pull it back and shuffle. The dealer had a Ten up, thus he had 20. I had hard 18; if I did nothing I was sure to lose.

I attempted to draw a card. As predicted, there was only one more card, a Ten, so the dealer pulled it back and shuffled. I attempted to draw again. When I saw the card I almost fell off my chair. It was a 3 for a total of 21 and a win. When the dealer turned up my cards he was astounded by my draw on hard 18. I was barely able to explain it away by seeming dazed and saying that I had added my cards to 15. When the same situation arose half an hour later, except that I held hard 19 against a sure 20, I did not dare draw seeking an Ace (to tie) or a Deuce (to win).

When there are other players at the table and you have not been able to see and count some of their cards by the time it is your turn to play, it is profitable, particularly near the end of the deck and when big bets are involved, to make inferences as to what these cards are and to use these inferences to modify your behavior. For example, suppose the count is (9,6) after you have seen the dealer's up card and your own cards, you are the fourth of four players, and the first three players stood (without hesitation) on their hole cards. Then the inference is quite strong that they each hold one and perhaps two Tens. Estimating their hole cards to be four Tens and two non-Tens, the true count, for purposes of your draw, is perhaps (7,2). Hence, if the dealer is showing an Ace and you hold hard 14, 15, or 16, you should draw, rather than stand. It is even likely that you should draw on hard 17 in this instance!

Learning the Strategy Tables

During the writing of this book, I taught the system to several people with diverse backgrounds and interests. One purpose was to see whether the card-counting methods and charts of this chapter, the key chapter in the first edition and the most difficult one, could readily be learned. Without exception, everyone was discouraged when he first saw Tables 8.3 and 8.4 and when he was told he would have to count the cards. Nearly everyone was surprised at the speed with which he learned. A couple of one-hour practice sessions, with someone else dealing, was generally enough to fix the basic strategy. Two more one-hour sessions were enough to teach the simplified Five-count system. By then almost everyone gets impatient with waiting for the relatively infrequent favorable (Fiveless) situations. Two to five additional one-hour practice sessions, plus some counting practice, are usually enough to teach the players to count the Tens and non-Tens, and to vary their bets accordingly (see Table 8.2), while they still play the basic strategy. The single remaining problem is memorizing one of the tables. We illustrate a method of memorization that has been worked out by experience.

The first logical step is to learn the parts of Table 8.3 that have to do with your big bets, namely those parts involving ratios of 2.25 or less (favorable decks). This information is given in Table 8.4, an approximation to Table 8.3 in which the precise Ten-count strategy is played for big bets and the basic strategy is played otherwise. One might think of Table 8.4 as the basic strategy plus some modifications.

Learn Table 8.4 in several stages.

Begin with the standing-numbers table; it is the most important. Like most tables in this book, this table is more easily learned if one looks for patterns in it. For instance, against 9, the change in ratio between squares is three tenths. Against 10, the changes are not very regular; in tenths, they are two, three, three, four. Note, however, that the standing number drops from 17 to 16 if the ratio drops to 2.2. A very slight excess of Tens is enough to change the standing number. In the Appendix we shall see that in the basic strategy the hard standing number against Ten is generally 16 for hands of 3 or more cards and barely 17 otherwise.

The table next in importance is hard doubling down.

There are not many pair-splitting squares to learn. However, the Ten splits are quite important. A player is ordinarily dealt a pair of Tens on about 1 hand in 11. The frequency is even higher when the ratio drops. Note that Ten splitting (and also Four splitting) occurs only against the favorable dealer's up cards of 2 through 6. Once again there is a sharp division between 6 and 7.

The soft-doubling-down table is the least important. It can be omitted or learned only approximately, if desired.

When most (or all) of Table 8.4 has been learned, the next stage is to get an approximate idea of the hard stand-

ing numbers against 2 through 6 when the ratio is high. You
probably already will have been "leaning" in these situations.

Further proficiency in the details of Table 8.3 are
for the expert.

Rate of Profit

By this time the reader should be wondering whether the
Ten-count strategy will win enough faster than the Five-
count strategy to justify the extra work involved in learning
and playing it. Table 8.5 illustrates the rate at which the Ten-
count system wins. The ratios were calculated and recorded
by a computer for 100,000 hands, and the results are
typical of what arises in actual play.

Table 8.5 is read as follows. If 25 cards are dealt off
the top of a well-shuffled pack (and counted by the player),
the player will find that a ratio of 1.0 or less will occur
only 0.1 per cent of the time. A ratio of 1.7 or less, but
above 1.6, will not occur at all. A ratio of 1.8 or less, but
above 1.7, will occur 14.5 per cent of the time. A ratio of
1.8 or less will occur 24.0 per cent of the time. (This last
figure is obtained by adding all figures in the 25-card
column up to and including the ratio for 1.7 to 1.8, namely,
0.1 + 0.5 + 2.0 + 6.9 + 14.5 = 24.0.)

Note from Table 8.5 that a player counting Tens has
an advantage of 1 per cent or more (i.e., a ratio of 2.0 or
less) about a third of the time. It turns out that the advantage ranges between 1 per cent in favor of the player and
1 per cent in favor of the house about a third of the time,
and that the house has an advantage of 1 per cent or more
about a third of the time.

When more than one player is at the table, the Tens
strategy loses somewhat in efficiency, but the decline is not
nearly as sharp as it is in the Fives strategy.

Study has shown that a scheme for betting that gives
very good protection against ruin while also providing a

TABLE 8.5. *Frequency of Favorable Situations Arising in the Ten-Count Strategy.**

Ratio Above	Ratio To	5	10	15	20	25	30	35	40	45	Average
	0.5										
0.5	1.0										0.3
1.0	1.1								0.1		2.5
1.1	1.2								0.5	1.6	0.1
1.2	1.3							1.2	2.0	9.5	1.0
1.3	1.4							3.7	6.9	23.2	0.1
1.4	1.5				0.1		1.9	9.8	14.5	29.5	4.9
1.5	1.6				0.8	0.4	5.6	18.1	21.7		3.2
1.6	1.7			0.1	4.0	9.7	13.3	23.6			0.8
1.7	1.8			1.3	10.6	17.6	21.8				2.1
1.8	1.9			6.3	19.4	26.6					4.7
1.9	2.0		2.3	15.6	24.2						4.2
2.0	2.1		9.8	24.4							9.3
2.1	2.2	14.6	24.7								5.1
2.2	2.3	36.0									9.3
2.3											3.3
		49.3	36.3	52.3	40.9	54.3	43.6	57.3	45.7	63.2	49.2

* These figures were obtained by having a computer shuffle and deal one deck 100,000 times. They are quite close to the expected values. Entries are to the nearest tenth of a per cent. Blank spaces are zeros. Columns sometimes do not total 100 per cent due to rounding off.

The situations arising near the end of the deck are often extremely favorable for the player. However, many casinos shuffle a few cards from the end. Hence we have not included any situations involving six or fewer cards remaining in the deck.

large yield is to risk a percentage of your initial capital equal to your percentage advantage. For example, with $200 and a 3 per cent advantage, bet $6; with a 10 per cent advantage, bet $20; with a 1 per cent advantage bet $2; with situations less favorable than 1 per cent, bet a minimum $1.

In the test of this system which I described in Chapter 5, modified proportional betting was used: 1-unit minimum when my advantage was below 1 per cent, 2 units with a 1 per cent advantage, 4 units with a 2 per cent advantage, and so on, up to 10 units with a 5 per cent advantage. Above 5 per cent all bets were leveled off at 10 units to reduce the possibility of frightening the casino. This precaution turned out to be insufficient in several of the casinos.

In the present era, with the widespread successful use of our methods in the casinos, bets should be limited to ratios of 1 to 5 or 1 to 3, or even kept constant!

There is a variation on the proportional betting schemes of the foregoing discussion that is mathematically superior to them but involves a little extra mental work. In it, the player bets an amount approximately proportional to his *current* capital. The amount bet should be equal to the player's percentage advantage. For example, suppose a player starts with $200. In a 10 per cent situation he bets $20. Suppose he later builds up to $300. He would now bet $30 in a 10 per cent situation.

It is not necessary to bet the precise amount called for in any of our betting schedules. The results do not vary significantly, even with considerable deviations from the suggested amounts.

Including Aces in the Count

Your results improve further if you adjust your bet size for an excess or shortage of Aces. When all the Aces are gone, subtract 4 per cent from your estimated advantage. When the deck has twice as many Aces as normal, add 4 per cent to your estimated advantage.

We use some extreme cases to illustrate how Aces can affect your advantage. Suppose the unused cards consist exclusively of Aces and Tens. (I have seen the last eight cards happen to be all Aces and Tens.) How much should you bet? If possible, bet one half of your capital; save the other half for pair splitting or insurance. If the dealer has an Ace up, you can insure and prevent him from winning in case he has blackjack.

If you lost your insurance, the dealer must have a pair of Aces and must bust when he draws; therefore you will win your main bet. If he has a Ten up, he may have an Ace under and, consequently, have blackjack. A part of the time you, too, will hold blackjack and the game will be a stand-off. The rest of the time you will lose, but this is the only time you lose. If the dealer has no blackjack, he has a Ten under also. Then with $(A,10)$ you win; with $(10,10)$ you can tie or, if any Aces remain, you can split your Tens with the chance of a net gain. With (A,A) you can split for a sure win if there are cards remaining. If the deck is exhausted, splitting (A,A) against the dealer's $(10,10)$ keeps your average loss fairly small.

The foregoing discussion is included to make it seem reasonable that when hands are dealt only from a collection of Aces and Tens, the player is greatly favored. A detailed mathematical analysis confirms this.

As you become comfortable with the Ten-count strategy, you can begin to keep track of Aces. When the deck has an excess of Aces, increase your bet somewhat over that which is called for in the straight Tens strategy. On the other hand, bets should be reduced when the deck has a scarcity of Aces (is Ace-poor.)

You must be more careful than ever, when counting Aces and Tens, to avoid letting the casino know that you are keeping track of the cards. The story of Junior illustrates what not to do. He was counting both Tens and Aces and betting heavily. After a while, he made a maximum (for him) bet of $200, since his count showed a very favorable situation. He was dealt a pair of Tens. There was still one Ace unseen. The dealer had a Ten showing but did not have a natural.

Junior had seen the burned card and knew that it was not an Ace. Since there was only one unused card left in the pack, it had to be the remaining Ace. Furthermore, this casino was at that time dealing the last card (the customary practice now is to withhold the last card and to place it with the used cards and shuffle). Now, placed in a situation such as this, knowing you would get the last card, an Ace, if you requested it, what would you do? Draw? Split the pair of Tens?

Junior asked to double down on his $200 bet. Pityingly, the dealer attempted to explain to this "foolish free spender" that he must have wanted to split his Tens. They argued until finally the pit boss was called over to settle the confusion. Now both the dealer and the pit boss pleaded with him, in an attempt to "save him from himself." By this time a crowd of employees as well as spectators had gathered. Finally, infuriated and exasperated from the long haggle, Junior yelled, "Give me the g-- d----d Ace!" The card was dealt. It was an Ace. The amazed pit boss paid the $400 and then escorted our hero to the door. Of course he was barred from further play in that casino.

The effect of Aces can be taken into account rather precisely. The idea is to estimate the relative Ace richness of the deck and then to add a correction to the advantage that is computed from the ratio of others to Tens. For example, suppose there are 26 cards remaining, all four Aces among them. The average number of Aces is two. The average number can be computed from $(26/52) \times 4$. Thus in this case the number is double the average so you *increase* your estimated advantage by 4 per cent. The general formula for the correction to your per cent edge, due to Ace richness or Ace poorness, is: $[13A/N\text{-}1] \times 4$ where A is the number of still unseen Aces and N is the total number of unused cards. A negative figure means the deck is Ace-poor and the player's advantage will be reduced (perhaps even eliminated altogether) by the negative correction.

It is difficult to make these additional calculations while playing the Tens strategy. I recommend that the reader who is counting Aces as well as Tens merely "lean in the indicated direction" rather than make a precise calculation.

The Remarkable Gain from Proper End Play

A few years ago, a now legendary figure, sometimes described as "the little dark-haired guy from Southern California" (we purposely avoid giving his name), approached a large and famous casino in Reno. The story goes that he explained he would like to play for large stakes—the house limit or more, if possible—and that he wanted a private game without publicity because he had tax problems. He set down carefully stipulated playing conditions that probably did not deviate from the spirit of the game. As a bachelor "steadily earning five figures," he had accumulated appreciable capital and was able, no doubt, to convince the casino that he had considerably more still. The house, thinking it had its usual advantage, was probably more than happy to accept these conditions.

Although I do not know the details of the proposition, it is not hard to make a reasonable guess as to what they were. From what I have learned through the grapevine, it seems likely that what I call end play (to be described below) was the main ingredient of this particular coup. If so, the conditions for the game would be as follows. The casino's usual rules, as to drawing and standing, doubling down, splitting, and insurance, are to be in force. In addition, from deal to deal, the player may *vary* at will both the number of hands he takes and the amounts he bets. Furthermore, the casino will deal down to the last card before shuffling. At first sight, this set of conditions seems pretty harmless. But before we see what happened at the casino

in question, let us examine play under these conditions
more closely.

Imagine, first, that seven cards, all Aces and Tens, remain to be played. What happens if you decide to take
exactly three hands? Then when you pick up your three
hands you find each one consists of either (A,A), $(A,10)$,
or $(10,10)$. The dealer, however, receives only one Ace or
one Ten, and since the deck runs out, he must shuffle before
getting his next card. You now have three powerful hands
facing him, and besides, he must draw his next card from
a deck that is poor in Aces and Tens. Generally, all three
of your hands win. The advantage frequently is 10 to 100
per cent in these situations. Money is won at a truly dizzy-
ing rate.

Here is an alternate variation. Suppose there are five
cards left, mostly Aces and Tens, and that you decide to
take five hands. Then you get all five of the cards in this
favored group, and the dealer gets none of them, for he
runs out of cards and must shuffle before dealing the first
card to himself. If you now get a Ten as your first card
this gives you a 15 to 20 per cent advantage; starting with
an Ace gives you a 35 to 40 per cent advantage.

If it happens instead that the end of the deck is very
poor in Aces and Tens, this too is to your advantage.
Suppose there are twelve small cards left. Take five hands
and place very small bets on each. All twelve cards are
used up in dealing the hands, and since mostly small cards
are involved, some cards will be drawn, forcing a shuffle.
When the deck is shuffled, twelve small cards are missing
and therefore the new cards will be dealt from a residue
whose ratio is 24/16 or 1.5. A few cards will be drawn,
but, although the ratio fluctuates in individual situations,
on the average it will also be 1.5 at the end of the round.
Thus by taking five hands to keep the small cards on the
table during the shuffle, the player has created a series of
highly favorable situations.

We now return to the story of what happened at the casino. The little dark-haired guy is said to have played for several successive nights. The first night he won ten or fifteen thousand dollars. Then, on successive nights he lost and won similar amounts. When the casino became accustomed to these large surges and when it was clear that they were primed to hang on even though they were well behind, he began playing to win. Hour after hour the money piled up. It is said that somewhere between $40,000 and $86,000, the casino "snapped" and called off the game. The latter figure is supposed to be the authentic one, but there are varying reports, probably because there were only four witnesses to the game—the player and three casino people. His idea of no publicity paid handsomely. During the next two years, the little dark-haired guy sold his proposition to other Nevada casinos. He was finally barred throughout the state after he had won more than $250,000.

Of course, since nearly every casino in Nevada now refuses to allow end play, the method is nearly dead. Many casinos are so intimidated that they will not set up private games. But keep it in mind. It paid off in the Puerto Rican casinos for several alert readers of the first edition.

9

Beating the Casino
Countermeasures

There is an abundance and variety of casino counter-measures. We cannot discuss all those in use at the time of this writing. Furthermore, as the players become more re-sourceful, so do the casinos, changing their countermeasures to meet new situations. The discussion of the principal countermeasures should make the player versatile enough to cope with new developments.*

Shuffle up

When I wrote the first edition I had the mistaken im-pression that the casinos could stop a system player by frequently reshuffling the deck. Let's consider the extreme case in which the game is played with one deck and that one deck is reshuffled at the end of each and every deal. Suppose

---

* An interesting book in connection with casino countermeasures is *Inside Nevada Gambling—Adventures of a Winning System Player* by Glenn L. Fraikin, Exposition Press, New York, $4.00. It tells of Fraikin's being barred, harrassed, forcibly ejected and embarrassed. You can generally avoid these problems if you are careful.

a player is alone at the table, playing one hand at a time. The best you can do, it may seem, is to use the basic strategy. Against the typical rules of Chapter 2, you will have an edge of about 0.13 per cent. For practical purposes, the game is even.

But suppose now that you take six hands, playing the whole table at once. On your first hand (if the cards are dealt down), you have seen only your hole cards and the dealer's up card. The situation is the same as before. But when it is time to play the second hand you have already seen the cards for the first hand. If you use the playing strategy for the complete point count or for the Ten count, you are able to play this hand better than if you stuck to the basic strategy. Naturally your advantage increases. You will win at an average rate that is greater than 0.13 per cent.

Things are better still on the third hand, and they are very good indeed, by the time you get to the sixth and last hand. You now have seen at least 13 and probably 18 or 20 cards. If you split some of the earlier hands, the figure could run much higher. Your average advantage, due to improvements in playing strategy, is roughly 1 per cent. This is about the same as the casino's edge in baccarat. You can make a big bet on the sixth hand of every deal. In fact, you could make a small bet on the first hand, a little larger bet on the second, and so on. The largest bet would be on the last hand.

Sitting in the last seat at a crowded table, you can make a big bet all the time if you generally see most of the cards played ahead of you. With cards dealt face up, as they are in Puerto Rico and in a number of the Nevada games, you see plenty of cards. There, in fact, from every seat you can see at least the players' hole cards, for an edge of 0.5 per cent or more.

In a casino where the cards are dealt face down, it may not be easy to see most of the cards before your turn to play. In fact, some casinos now use shills and have them conceal their cards. The dealer rakes in their cards without ever showing them. You can prevent the shills from playing, and make sure you see everyone's cards, by filling the table with your cooperative friends first. (They can play the basic strategy, have fun, and break even, if nothing else.)

Dealers Who Count

After *Beat the Dealer* became a national best seller and several hundred thousand people read it, some casinos had their employees read it. Then some of the dealers were taught to count. There were two ideas behind this. First, these dealers could help spot count players (more on this later). Secondly, these dealers could shuffle up when the deck went good but keep dealing if it went bad.

Suppose a dealer does this. What do you do? The only solution that I have found, besides looking for another and better game, is to sit in the last seat. Bet heavily on the first deal and hope you win with your 1 per cent edge. Bet lightly otherwise. If you pull ahead (and the odds favor you, but not tremendously), your dealer may give up his tactics.

Strike When the Deck Is Hot

We have just seen how dealers can shuffle away the good cards and keep playing with bad cards. You can do very much the same thing. Suppose you are about to enter a game. Stop. Don't sit down. Get your count first. And be sure you have some casino chips in your hand. Now wait until the count is good. Then pull up a seat and toss your *large* bet down. This way you always start your game with a good deck. You are striking when the deck is hot.

This is a very nice way to pick up extra change when you are on your way through your hotel's gaming areas. The dealer generally doesn't reshuffle on you: he doesn't know yet that this first bet of yours is going to turn out to be "large."

Punishing Fakes

Many dealers reshuffle when you increase your bet. A few of these are legitimate Ten counters and know that the deck has gone "good." But most of them are not. They just reshuffle to be safe against system players. And a good many of the ones I've played against are out-and-out fakes. That is, they pretend (either to the players or to their pit boss) that they are counting Tens and non-Tens. When a big bet goes out, they reshuffle. But actually they have no idea what the count is.

When you find a fake, stay with him. He is "money in the bank." Here is what you do. Start by making a big bet (3 to 5 units). When the deck goes bad, increase your bet, and when he reshuffles, pull back the extra amount. When the deck stays neutral or goes good, keep your bet the same. The result is that the dealer shuffles away the bad decks. You always play against average or good decks. You have a consistent advantage and probably win.

Multiple Decks

There has been some increase in the number of blackjack games played with either two or four decks. Some casinos believe that it is much more difficult to count several decks. You will find it a little more work. But if you are fairly good with one deck, you shouldn't have much trouble.

The most serious drawback to two or four decks is that the advantage for various values of the high-low index or the Ten-count ratio are not quite as large. They are roughly 0.4 per cent less for two decks and 0.5 per cent less for four decks. Also, the deviations from normal deck composition are smaller. So there are somewhat fewer favorable situations, and the ones that occur are less favorable. If the casino were to reshuffle two or even four decks after every deal, even sitting in the sixth seat wouldn't help. But the casinos won't do this. The game would slow down to such a crawl that bored players would keep drifting away.

Multiple decks have one big advantage for the player who strikes when the decks are hot. When two decks, or better four decks, go good, they stay good much longer. So when you sit down to a good situation with a big bet, things are likely to stay good for a while. This partly camouflages your actions.

Rules Changes

The gambling world was electrified on April 1, 1964. The Las Vegas Resort Hotel Association announced that the rules of blackjack were being changed [34]. This was the first time in history that the rules of a major casino gambling game had been significantly altered. The rules changes were made to combat the winning blackjack systems (primarily the Ten-count) introduced in the first edition of *Beat the Dealer*. In the words of Gabriel Vogliatti, a spokesman for the Las Vegas Resort Hotel Association [45]: "In the last 15 years there hasn't been one plane that landed without at least one person in possession of a system. This guy [Thorp] is the first in Las Vegas history to have a system that works."

The specific rules changes forbade the splitting of Aces and restricted doubling down to totals of hard 11 only. As you see from Table 9.1, the effect is to reduce the basic-strategy player's advantage by roughly 1 per cent. The reduction is somewhat larger in favorable situations and somewhat smaller in unfavorable ones. Thus a situation which was a 10 per cent advantage, for example, is reduced to a little less than 9 per cent. Clearly the point-count and Ten-count methods will still uncover favorable situations. But there won't be quite as many, and they won't be quite as good.

How did the rules changes affect the system players?

The good players went right back the next day and continued winning. True, their rate of winning was cut somewhat. But it wasn't enough to cheer up the casinos.

Against casinos with unfavorable rules, the betting scale should be adjusted downward. Perhaps the simplest method is to decrease all large bets by one unit. Alternately, if you use the point-count system without strategy refinements, you can simply decrease your initial count by one point per deck in use. For example, in a two-deck game with poor rules (such as is played in Puerto Rico and in some spots in Nevada), start with a point-count total of -2 instead of 0. Then play precisely as before.

TABLE 9.1. *The Effect of the (Temporary) Las Vegas Rules Changes.*

		Basic strategy old rules	Basic strategy new Las Vegas rules
	Player's overall advantage*	.0013	−.0089
Player's	A#	−.0847	−.0853
advantage	A*	−.3603	−.3607
when	2	.1011	.0888
dealer's	3	.1376	.1219
up	4	.1844	.1626
card	5	.2369	.2073
is	6	.2425	.2121
	7	.1464	.1374
	8	.0547	.0490
	9	−.0437	−.0471
	10*	−.1706	−.1717
	10#	−.1032	−.1044

\# Excluding the possibility that dealer has a natural.
* Including the possibility that dealer has a natural.

The casino operators had read as far as Chapter 5 (Ten count), but they had not read as far as Chapter 8 (Rules Variations), which explained how to counter their rules changes. Further, I predicted when I wrote the first edition two years earlier that rules changes would be tried and that they would not be effective. But the casinos hadn't read that far yet. It took them two or three weeks to throw in the sponge and go back to the old rules. What was the trouble? A sharp young journalist named Jude Wanniski explained it very clearly in a by-lined article in the *National Observer*:

> Overnight, play at the Las Vegas blackjack tables fell off. In fact, play at all the gaming tables declined as the flow of tourists into the city diminished. Casino employees, whose income depends in large part on the number of tips they receive, began screaming that the new blackjack rules were a bane to the industry.
>
> First one casino, then another, quietly scuttled the new rules. By last week, Las Vegas gamblers threw in the towel. They admitted they'd rather have all their business back, even if it meant putting up with the system players.

Rules Variations

In light of the attempted Nevada rules changes and the considerable variations in blackjack as played throughout the world, the reader should be prepared to estimate the effect of any deviations from the typical rules of Chapter 2. You can do this by consulting Table 9.2. To the basic-strategy edge of 0.12 per cent for the player, add or subtract the correction indicated by the table for each rules variation being used. The final result is the overall player advantage (if positive) or casino advantage (if negative).

At various points in the book we discussed the variations in England, Puerto Rico, and Nevada. One rule, which is apparently peculiar to the Far East, has not been considered. It is called "surrender."

In the Far East, particularly in Macao (a Portuguese colony that is a short hydrofoil ride from Hong Kong) and Manila, the blackjack rules are like those of Chapter 2 except that doubling down is permitted only with a two-card total of 11. But the player is offered the additional strategy option of surrender. At any time, unless the dealer is showing an Ace, the player may "surrender" his hand, retaining one half of the amount of his bet and losing the other half. Braun estimates that with best play surrender gains about 0.15 per cent for the player. This is more than offset by the player's loss of about 0.8 per cent because of the restrictions on doubling down.

TABLE 9.2. *Approximate Effect of Common Rules Variations on Player's Advantage When the Basic Strategy Is Used.*

Rules variations	Player's loss or gain (in per cent)
forbid doubling down on	
hard 11	−0.89
hard 10	−0.56
hard 9	−0.14
hard 8	−0.00
all soft totals	−0.14
all totals after pair splitting	−0.13
allow doubling down on any three cards	0.19*
allow doubling down on any number of cards	0.20*
four decks	−0.51
two decks	−0.35
dealer draws to soft 17	−0.20
dealer draws only to soft 17 with Ace up	−0.23
dealer drawing to soft 17 is optional	−(0.23+)
further splitting of pairs	
all pairs, one deck	0.053
all pairs, two decks	.08
all pairs, four decks	0.11 (est.)
all pairs except Aces, two decks	.04
all pairs, one deck, and unlimited draw to split Aces	.037
all pairs, two decks, and unlimited draw to split Aces	.06
and double on hard 11 only	.05
all pairs except Aces	0.024
drawing any number of cards to split Aces	0.14
no splitting of Aces	−0.16
no splitting of Aces and no doubling down on soft 12	−0.16
forbid pair splitting	−0.46
two-to-one pay-off for blackjack	2.32
Puerto Rican rules, one deck	−0.71
two decks	−1.04
Surrender (Macao, Manila)	0.15 (est.)

* These figures are from [2,3]. A more precise result can be computed from the tables in the Appendix.

Camouflage

The casinos have become painfully aware of the thousands of basic-strategy players who do not lose money. Even worse, they are infested with hundreds of good Ten-count players who carry off money. These good players, particularly, have a problem. When they become known to the casinos, they find shuffle up, or the dealer hiding cards. Sometimes they are barred (asked to leave the casino). Or they run into heavy cheating (sometimes undisguised!).

Clearly, if you want to be left alone to play a good game of blackjack, you must disguise your play. First, do not start at the beginning of every fresh deck with a small bet. With one-deck games and typical rules (so I have a slight edge off the top), I get best results by betting large off the top of the deck almost half the time. Of course, if you glimpse a burned or bottom card, you can choose these times more effectively. Dealers think, "If he's going to bet big off the top of the deck, shuffle up is a waste of time."

In casinos with two or more dealers or less favorable rules, you ought to bet big off the top much less frequently.

The size of your bets is also important. I have played against dealers who thought it was natural to bet a $5 chip or a $25 chip but not natural to carefully bet $5, $10, $15, $20, or $25, depending on the deal. So I bet $5 except when things were moderately good. Then I bet $25. In Puerto Rico I bet $1 while waiting and $50 in all favorable situations, since nothing bothered them! You must learn what is best in your situation. A ratio of 1 to 5 or even 1 to 3 in bet sizes might be a good beginning while you explore the situation. A ratio of 1 to 2 is acceptable. Against one deck and typical rules, a ratio of 1 to 1 is acceptable (all bets the same!) if you sit in fifth or sixth seat at a full table and can see most of the cards before your turn!

Disguises

As a result of the intense publicity and the wide distribution of my picture, I have lately found it nearly

impossible to get a reasonable game. As a last resort, I grew
a beard for the summer and got used to contact lenses. Then
I spent four days in Las Vegas, Reno, and Lake Tahoe. In
the beginning I wore the full beard. My usual glasses were
replaced by contact lenses and sweep-around sunglasses.
After I had won for two days in Las Vegas, players with
beards began to receive most unfriendly treatment. Two
companions and I went on to Reno and Lake Tahoe. We
walked into a crowded casino on the north shore of Lake
Tahoe (famed for gangland connections). There were no
seats at the blackjack tables. Then a boss looked up and
saw the bearded apparition. His jaw dropped. He called in
a dealer and opened up a table. I sat down. Two toughs
trotted up and plopped down on either side of me.

My companions (I NEVER travel alone in Nevada)
thought I was about to be hurled from the casino.

The two toughs, the dealer, and I played on in complete silence for ten minutes or so. When I was absolutely
sure the dealer was a cheat, I walked away. The two toughs
immediately trotted off. The dealer closed up the table and
went off to wait for the next problem. A minute later, all
was as before. The throngs of happy, fun-loving tourists
went on with their merrymaking. Not one of them had been
the least bit aware of the little drama that had taken place
before them.

It looked as if bearded players were through. But it
had taken me four weeks to grow the beard and I was
determined to use it one more time. After further adventures
we arrived in Reno.

At about 3 A.M. I began to play at a club in downtown
Reno (about 50 or 60 miles from the scene in Tahoe). The
club was well known for its fair rules and for dealing down
to the last card. I always collect a few hundred dollars from
this club whenever I am in Reno, whatever befalls me elsewhere. This club doesn't seem to be "in" with the other
owners. In particular, I thought they would not have heard
in advance of the bearded threat.

My table was full. There was no opportunity for end play. But I knew from past experience that this casino wouldn't allow that anyhow. I played on, betting $5 to $25, the maximum size and spread of bets that I felt would be tolerated here. I won steadily. The casino plied me liberally with strong drinks. I gave the casino people the impression that I was careless, woozy, and a bad player. "Doubling down on Five—ridiculous; and winning, too. What can you do about luck like that? But it will run out. It's bound to."

But the cards ran well and instead of winning an expected $25 to $75 in an hour, I piled up $300. So the casino personnel paraded by, one after another. They scrutinized me, watched my play, and examined my face. At the end of an hour they had all examined me. They had had enough. A hostile brunet pit boss (the same one who saw me practice for eight hours in the same club when I first played in Reno; see Chapter 5) now took over as dealer. She smiled pleasantly. She dealt the first hand: blackjack to herself. I was watching for the second deal (see Chapter 10) and caught it, and I got up. Purring cattily, she invited me to stay on and play.

During the previous hour of playing, I had a single dealer. (This casino leaves the dealers on at one table interminably, but this first one couldn't cheat). She was a young blond, lonely, emotionally troubled, and in search of a man. When she glimpsed the stack of $100 bills in my wallet, she became exceedingly friendly. She was disappointed and upset to be so abruptly parted from her fish.

The blond told me (wonderful fellow that I was) that she hated beards and "everything would be all right if I shaved it off." So it occurred to me that I could later make a perfect test of my disguise.

The next evening I shaved off the ragged full-length beard. The only clue to my having had it was an unusual paleness about certain parts of my face. Instead of careless casual clothes, I now wore a suit. I removed the sweep-around sunglasses and wore only my contact lenses. I combed my hair somewhat differently. I was ready for the test.

I called for my companions, who had never seen me sans beard. When they answered the door, they did not recognize me. Instead of an aging unkempt man of forty-five, I was a springy, crew-cut young executive of twenty-five, out for an evening on the town.

When 3 A.M. approached, I left the game I was in and went to the casino where the blond dealt. There she was, at the same table, and there was one vacant seat. I sat down and began to play. There was no glimmer of recognition on her face.

Again I bet $5 to $25, with chips I had been careful to purchase in advance from the cashier, with a few carefully preserved small bills. There was no evidence of the previous evening's stack of hundreds to give my dealer a clue. I did not talk, I only gestured (not too unusual a behavior pattern). When the waitresses came to ply me with drinks, I whispered "milk." The dealer could not hear my voice. After two milks, the waitresses didn't bother me.

So far, my disguise seemed to be working perfectly. But chance soon put it to a real test. The cards ran well again and I began to pile up winnings at almost the same rate as the evening before. Next, the player on my left (I was in fifth seat, my usual choice, since the casinos expect system players to be in sixth seat) turned out to be a cheat! He would pile his bet carelessly on the layout. Then he would check his hole cards. Then he would try to sneak some extra silver dollars onto the layout if he thought he had a good hand. If he thought he had a poor hand he would try to remove some of his bet. The dealer didn't know what to do. Then the same parade of casino personnel filed by to examine the cheat.

The bosses watched him play for a few minutes. He was such a bad player that, even though he was cheating,

he was barely breaking even. They gave orders to leave
him alone!

Both the cheat and I had been carefully scrutinized by
the same gang that had studied me the previous night. No
one recognized me. But after an hour, and another $300,
their patience wore thin. As on the night before, the cheating dealer came in. I left.

Disguises do work. They are a lot of trouble, but they
can be fun, too.

The Automatic Blackjack Machines

One of the most interesting casino countermeasures is
the recent introduction of automatic (electronic) blackjack
machines to replace the dealers. The machines have been
or are being tried at several casinos. The text of an adver-
tisement on pages 137–8 gives the details.

Let's use our methods to analyze the form of automatic
blackjack presented in the ad.

Notice first that the machine deals a one-deck game
and reshuffles after every deal. This goes a long way toward
negating the gains from card counting. Our first impulse is
to sit in the last seat and use the cards we see to get an
edge (as explained on pages 124–126). But there are only
four seats. So the advantage gained will be considerably
less, probably about 0.33 to 0.5 per cent.

The next thing to notice is how the rules differ from
our typical rules. First, doubling down is restricted to hard
totals of 10 or 11. Secondly, pair splitting is not allowed.
Both these restrictions on the player increase the house
edge. According to Table 9.2, there is a loss of 0.41 per
cent due to the restriction on doubling down on hard 8,
hard 9, the soft totals, and after pair splitting. The loss due
to no pair splitting is 0.47 per cent. Thus the basic strategy
would appear to yield an advantage to the player of 0.13
per cent, reduced by 0.88 per cent, or a net advantage to
the casino of 0.75 per cent.

"AUTOMATIC BLACKJACK"

is a gaming machine manufactured in the state of Nevada.

"AUTOMATIC BLACKJACK" is electronically operated using a full simulated fifty-two-card deck—automatically shuffled and dealt. Play is initiated upon the deposit of a coin, or coins, in any or all denominations of quarters, halves or silver dollars ... to a limitation of five coins of each denomination.

The sequence of the game is in accord with all standard "BLACKJACK" or "21" games.

The player has the option of "hitting or standing" on the hand and score dealt. ALL SCORES ARE NUMERICALLY INDICATED IMMEDIATELY.

The "dealer" will continue to draw cards automatically until it has a score of 17 or more—at this time the score of the player is compared to the "dealer" and payoff is automatically made according to the score and the amount of the bet made. If the player makes a "BLACKJACK" he receives double his original bet instead of the usual one and a half payoff.

"AUTOMATIC BLACKJACK" is fully approved by the Nevada Gaming Commission. All card dealing is absolutely uncontrolled and based upon chance.

Any player, after receiving two or more cards showing a score of 10 or 11 may elect to "DOUBLE DOWN." Simply press the yellow flashing light button, increase your bet in the same denomination up to double your original bet, press the "HIT" button, and you will receive one card only to complete your hand.

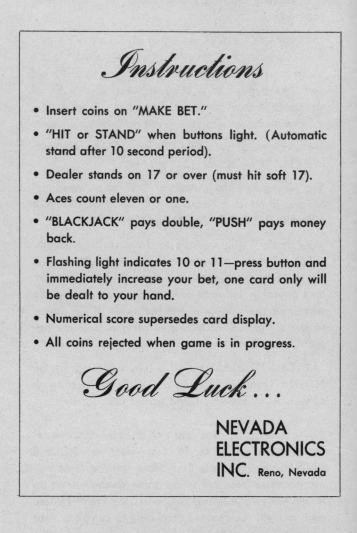

Instructions

- Insert coins on "MAKE BET."

- "HIT or STAND" when buttons light. (Automatic stand after 10 second period).

- Dealer stands on 17 or over (must hit soft 17).

- Aces count eleven or one.

- "BLACKJACK" pays double, "PUSH" pays money back.

- Flashing light indicates 10 or 11—press button and immediately increase your bet, one card only will be dealt to your hand.

- Numerical score supersedes card display.

- All coins rejected when game is in progress.

Good Luck ...

NEVADA ELECTRONICS INC. Reno, Nevada

Notice also that a player sitting in the fourth seat would ordinarily have an occasional profitable insurance bet, provided he knew the hole cards of at least one of the other three people at the table. (The player must see at least five cards of a complete deck before there is a possibility of a ratio below 2.00 and a profitable insurance bet. Two players' hole cards and the dealer's up card are sufficient.) But this little advantage does not apply here, for insurance is not offered.

There is one more rules change. If the player receives blackjack *and the dealer does not* (the ad doesn't say this but presumably it means it) he wins twice his original bet instead of the usual one and a half times it. Clearly this helps the player. How much? The chance (in a one-deck game) that a specified player will get blackjack *and* the dealer will not is 4.649 per cent. But the player now wins an extra 50 per cent each time this happens. So the net gain to the player, due to this rule, is 50% × 4.649%, or 2.32 per cent. So the player's gain with the basic strategy is increased from −0.75 per cent to + 1.57 per cent.

This is a tidy rate of profit for each and every hand. So a *basic-strategy* player should make a steady profit. One drawback is the fact that the machine will accept bets only up to a total of $8.75 per hand. But at 100 hands per hour one *should* expect an average profit of $8.75 × 100 × 1.57% or over $13 per hour!

The ad reproduced here was picked up in Reno and in Lake Tahoe. Recent information from Las Vegas is that the machines there all pay 1.5 to 1 for blackjack. Further, this is rounded off to the nearest quarter, *against the player*. For example, a 25¢ bet receives only 25¢ for a natural, not 37½¢. But a 50¢ bet receives 75¢ for a natural. Clearly the player should only bet in multiples of 50¢ against such a machine. Even so, the edge is now an unfavorable 0.75 per cent.

Warning: Machines wear out or become defective. Also, an unscrupulous person could set an automatic blackjack machine to cheat. Before I would play such a machine, I would tally 1000 or so dealt cards to see if appropriate proportions of each type of card were being dealt. I would further keep track of the percentage gain that a player experiences in 1000 hands or so. You are better off doing this by watching than playing.

The Paper Route Technique

The questions I have been asked most often is, "Can a player using your system still win in Nevada, after all the publicity and reader successes?" and "What is the best way to do this?" Yes, you can go on winning in Nevada. Here is a technique which is very effective. Before you begin a session of play, set aside from your stake an amount equal to about 5 large bets—perhaps 20 or 25 units. Play until you either lose this amount or win this amount. Do not show the 20 or 25 units at once, but instead buy chips from it as required. If you play for an hour, stop anyhow.

The point is this. If you play no more than an hour, you are less likely to attract attention or be remembered. If you lose no more than 20 or 25 units in a session, no one cheating dealer can ruin you. If you win no more than 20 or 25 units, you are less likely to be acted against as a possible threat because of your winnings. "He was just a little lucky this time but we'll get him next time."

Remember your dealers. Return to the dealers you do well against. Avoid the dealers you lose 20 or 25 units to. This way you never get cheated twice by the same dealer. You may lose legitimately and then avoid an honest dealer. This can't be helped.

The method is oversimplified to illustrate principles. Make appropriate modifications for your situation. After a session, you should go to another casino. When you are using the method, you stroll from casino to casino, collecting money, much as a newsboy for a paper route goes from door to door.

10

How to Spot Cheating

Blackjack dealers in casinos are often fantastically skillful with cards. Before I became seriously interested in blackjack, I and everyone I knew believed that although dealers could cheat if they so desired, they did not cheat. The well-publicized argument is that the casinos enjoy a natural advantage in the game and will win anyhow. Why should a casino risk possible exposure and the resultant bad publicity, loss of customers, and perhaps even loss of their gaming license? Alternatively, why would a crooked dealer who works for an honest casino risk losing his job in order to line his pockets?

We might answer this with another question: "Isn't there widespread corruption in political life and in the business world? And isn't it usually for the same stakes (money) and with comparable risks (loss of position or of license to operate, bad publicity, etc.)? Why then should legalized gambling be more immune from dishonesty than 'legalized' business?"

In recent years it has become public knowledge that

prominent gangster groups (such as the Mafia and the Cosa Nostra) are behind a number of the casinos, including some of the largest ones. Pulitzer-prize-winning writer Ed Reid and coauthor Ovid Demaris detail the grisly story in *The Green Felt Jungle*. Mob control in Nevada reaches everywhere, even to the highest levels. The book is "must" reading for anyone who visits Nevada. Other details can be found in [17, 24, 28, 33, 46, 51].

Reid and Demaris tell how casino mobsters, in various falling-outs, blew each other apart. Not only do the mobsters fatten their tills with "legitimate" profits from their casinos; they also take money "off the top." That is, they habitually report a smaller gross than is actually received. An account of these practices was given by Wallace Turner in a series of articles in the *New York Times*, November 18-22, 1964.

Now let me ask you again, are men of the Cosa Nostra, who bribe public officials, who steal money off the top, who help to finance their rackets (dope, prostitution, and smuggling) with their casino profits, who commit murder to settle their differences—are these men going to stop short at a little cheating at cards? Perhaps they are good sports. Perhaps they don't want the extra profits that come from cheating, especially when the "suckers" won't have a chance in a million of spotting the cheating—and who, if they did spot it, wouldn't be able to do anything about it.

Before we continue, let me try to set things in perspective. In the great majority of blackjack games there is no cheating. But there is enough cheating (I estimate the average player will face a cheat perhaps 5 or 10 per cent of the time) to make it a serious problem. It can mean the difference between winning and losing. So we must understand how to minimize our losses from cheating.

I was originally naïve enough to swallow the argument that blackjack as played in the casinos is generally honest.

It took painful personal experience to convince me otherwise. The first such experience was not long in coming.

The Knockout Dealer: A Stubborn Expert Wastes $20,000 in a Single Night

One afternoon during the test of the system in Nevada, Mr. X went off alone to play the Tens strategy. Early the next morning he told me he had played steadily for eight to ten hours at one of the large hotels. He made house-limit bets of $500 in sufficiently favorable situations, and at the end of a few hours he had won $13,000. At this point the hotel brought in its "knockout" dealer—a cheat employed specifically to dispose of big winners.

Her method of cheating was to peek at the top card when it came time for her to draw to her own hand. If she liked the top card, she dealt it (honestly) to herself. If she did not like it, she dealt herself the card just below the top card, commonly referred to as the "second." Even though she did not know what the second was, it was a better risk than the top card about half the time.

Mr. X stubbornly played on, hoping he could beat the cheat anyhow. The cheat faced him for forty minutes at a time. Then she rested for twenty minutes during which time the game was honest again. Mr. X hoped to win more in the tweny-minute sessions than he would be cheated out of in the forty-minute sessions. But he made a fatal error. He continued to bet on a large scale against the knockout dealer, rather than reducing his bets to a few dollars and waiting until she had to be relieved. Thus he lost too heavily against her. After a few hours he had lost back $20,000, cancelling his $13,000 lead and putting him $7,000 in the hole. When Mr. X complained to the owner, a person who was responsible for the operation of several large casinos, he explained that a (mythical?) Texan had won $17,000 the day before and the casino could not afford further losses.

The Queen of Hearts

Anxious to learn to protect myself from being cheated I visited this particular casino the next morning, accompanied by Mr. Y. Mr. X had described the knockout dealer to us: a thinnish, grim-faced woman of about forty, with black hair that was beginning to gray.

I purchased $1,000 worth of chips from the cashier and seated myself at the nearest table. I bet $30 and then the dealer dealt a card to me and one to herself. As she dealt the second card to me, the pit boss rushed over, stopped her, took the cards, and called over a dealer to replace her. The new dealer was a thinnish, grim-faced woman of about forty whose black hair was beginning to turn gray.

I received a pair of Eights and the dealer had a Three showing. I split my Eights and got totals of 20 and 18. The dealer's hole card was a Ten. Mr. Y and I watched as the dealer, holding the deck edge up, bent the top card back slightly to see what it was. We saw it too: the Queen of Hearts. That would have busted her so she dealt the second card to herself. It was an Eight, giving her 21, and she raked in our $60. Angrily Mr. Y spelled out for her what she had done. She reddened and looked down. She said nothing and pretended not to hear our loud, angry protests. When the pit boss came over, he also showed no reaction. There was nothing we could do—"it was our word against hers." We left, poorer but wiser.

After that experience and before writing this chapter, I went on several exploratory trips with the purpose of investigating cheating. I played at most of the major casinos in Las Vegas and Reno for periods ranging from a few minutes (cheating) to several hours, with bets ranging from $1 to $125. I was cheated frequently enough to learn to classify and spot a dozen or so current techniques. There was cheating at large plush casinos, as well as at smaller out-of-the-way places. There was cheating at all betting levels, even for 25¢!! In many additional instances, the cards behaved so strangely that I suspected cheating although I could not actually see seconds being dealt (with a good dealer it is extremely difficult to see).

On both the Reno-Tahoe trip and the first Las Vegas trip (taken four months after the Reno-Tahoe trip), I had the good fortune to be accompanied by individuals who were able to play the Ten-count strategy, who were expert both at demonstrating and spotting dealer cheating and who patiently instructed me in the ways in which the dealer can cheat. Furthermore, since each of these individuals had money invested in the play, they were always at my side, watching attentively.

I emphasize that the cheating incidents described are my personal experiences. I do not wish to imply that they are necessarily representative. The average amount of cheating is certainly less than the amount encountered by a well-identified "prime target" like me. In addition, it probably varies with such things as changes in government, casino management, and ownership, and with the size of bets, the time of day, and the individual dealer.

In some cases an honest casino may unknowingly hire a dishonest dealer. This dealer could cheat the house by letting a friend win heavily. If the house checks receipts regularly, they might notice that the given dealer frequently has unusually poor shifts. In order to prevent detection, a logical cover-up by the dealer is to cheat other players to make up the deficit. Some people describe this behavior of the dealer as a Robin Hood function.

I emphatically do not wish to imply that one part of Nevada is more or less free from cheating than any other part. I also believe that the cheating problem is not so great that people should completely refrain from playing. However, anyone who does play blackjack should learn without delay some of the elementary ways in which his opponent can cheat. (Sad to say, this advice applies equally to the other card games, both casino and private.)

I have been told by a reliable source that in the

first five years of the Nevada Gaming Control Board's
operation, they closed down more than twenty casinos for
cheating. Little if any publicity (exception: [71]) was
generally given to these proceedings, and the casinos usually
reopen promptly under new management.

The amount of cheating varies from almost none to
over 90 per cent, depending on which area of the world you
are playing in. There is a similar variation in the amount of
help the authorities will give to a player who has been
cheated, varying from no help at all to a great deal. You
may wish to investigate the conditions in your area before
you play.

There are dozens of ways to cheat at blackjack and at
card games in general. All we can do here is sketch some
of the more popular ones, based on my experience with the
casinos.

Marked Cards

One main technique in cheating is for the dealer to
identify the top card in order to deal a second, if it is
advantageous, at some appropriate point in the game. The
simplest way of identifying a card from its back is to mark
on the back, in some kind of code, just what the card is. A
marked deck is called "paper." Millions of decks of marked
cards are produced annually and are readily purchased by
mail from supply houses specializing in crooked gambling
equipment. They are also available in most "magic" stores.

All the most widely used standard brands are available. There is no safety in the fact that a pack may have
been manufactured by a reputable company; someone else
can easily "mark" the deck. For example, anyone can
purchase at nominal cost special inks and brushes for
this purpose. For the details of how cards are marked,
pictures of marked cards, and some of the styles of mark-
ing, the reader is referred to [15, 21, 22, 36, 53, 58, 66].
Photographs illustrating second dealing (discussed below),
also appear in some of these references.

On one occasion I was betting from $2 to $20 while a card expert stood by to protect me against possible cheating. A short while after I began to play, the deck was taken out and a new one was brought in. I requested the old deck as a souvenir. I wanted it in order to check for markings. Even though I insisted on that particular deck, the casino refused to give it to me and instead, after much hunting and digging, produced another deck. The latter was in considerably better condition than the one they had refused to give up. Suspicious, I continued to play against the new deck, and as I was winning moderately—there was a tremendous streak of favorable situations—my suspicions were lulled. After about thirty minutes I stopped and my friend told me that I was playing against a marked deck. He said that both of the dealers against whom I played dealt seconds whenever called for if the bets were $10 or more, and not otherwise. Immediately an odd incident came to mind. Once a card stuck in the deck, held only by its corner. It did not come loose until the dealer flicked his wrist sharply. The card must have been a second, for it was hanging there and was held both above and below by other cards in the deck.

My friend said he did not pull me out of the game because I was winning anyhow. Although I did win something, my winnings were only a small part of what they might have been with such tremendously favorable situations as had occurred.

Frequently dealers of seconds have the habit of "kicking" the wrist of the hand that is holding the deck as part of their motion of dealing. This helps prevent cards from getting stuck and hanging as in the above incident. Thus when you see a dealer who has this otherwise unnecessary motion, you should suspect very strongly that he is able to deal seconds.

One of the cheat dealers, who had worked for the casinos on 24-hour call, showed me a novel card-marking method. He took his thumbnail and pressed the backs of Aces and Tens on their top edge. He did not scratch them but rather merely rounded them slightly; when this was done the cards seemed no different from the others in the deck, as several friends and I learned when we hunted for the markings. However, when the deck was held at a certain angle to the light, the edges of the marked cards gleamed just enough so that a trained eye could pick them out. Because of the angles involved in light reflection, when the dealer can see the gleam, no one else can.

This dealer claimed the Gaming Control Board had at different times confiscated several decks which he had so marked and that images of them had been projected greatly enlarged on a wall without the markings ever having been detected.

Some people fall asleep at night thinking about their jobs, or their stocks, or their families. Mathematicians fall asleep thinking out problems in higher mathematics. Some people just count sheep. But this dealer confided that he and his friends fall asleep thinking up "new ways to cheat 'em."

Peeking

Marked cards have the disadvantage of being concrete evidence that can be used in a court of law. A more common method of identifying the top card, which has the further advantage that it may be used with any deck whatsoever, is for the dealer to actually look at the face of the top card. This is called peeking.

A skilled dealer can peek at the top card in plain view of a tableful of players with almost no risk of being caught. Suppose that a player busts. The dealer collects his chips and his cards. He will often use both hands for this. If he holds the deck in the left hand, as that hand reaches out, it is natural to turn it over so the deck is upside down. Try this and freeze your left hand in this partially extended position. Now reach out with your right hand and bend the right rear corner down slightly. Notice that you can identify the card by the exposed part of its face but that this portion of the card is not visible to someone sitting across the table. Now, certainly no one is going to reach across with his other hand and bend down the card. But a skilled dealer can accomplish this swiftly and invisibly with the same hand with which he holds the deck. Fortunately many if not most of the cheats seem to be much less practiced at peeking than they are at second dealing, so if you are watchful, you can often catch them as they peek.

If you are suspicious, there is one method which will frequently catch the peeking or put a stop to it. If the dealer peeks, his eyes must rest upon the card at which he is peeking unless he uses a "shiner." While one person plays, another person stands (this has advantages over sitting, as we shall see when we discuss dealing seconds) behind the player and stares at the dealer's eyes. Whenever the dealer's eyes look at the deck, the watcher's eyes flick down to the deck to see if a peek was possible and then flick back to the dealer's eyes. The watcher should also have his eyes on the deck whenever a card is being dealt.

I have found this technique extremely successful. Some cheat dealers become so tense and nervous about being caught that they become clumsy and are caught all the more quickly. Others stop cheating altogether under the pressure.

A "shiner" is a little concealed mirror with which the dealer sees the faces of the cards, before or as they are dealt. It might be put in such places as the face of a ring, the inside of a pipe bowl, or the polished edge of the money tray [53].

A Simple Home Experiment

Suppose that the dealer peeks and deals seconds at will. Here is a simple home experiment to show you the enormous average advantage he gains whenever he decides to do this.

Deal out one hand to a single player (imaginary, if

necessary) and one to yourself, as dealer. Have the player use the basic strategy. Each time, before you give a card to the player or yourself, peek at the top card. (It is easier simply to deal from a face-up pack, with all cards left up on the table.) If you prefer not to deal that card, hold it and deal the second card. A certain amount of judgment is required here. When you feel your judgment is good, make an initial bet of one chip on each hand. Record the results for one hundred hands. Shuffle the deck well each time you need to reshuffle. I tried 100 hands against a player using the basic strategy. The player won 9 units and the dealer won 110. The net gain for the dealer was a whopping +101 per cent. Compare with the results expected for 100 honest hands, given in Table 3.6.

Dealing Seconds

Dealing seconds is the principle weapon of literally millions of card cheats throughout the world. When competently done, it is almost invisible, even to experts. Sleight of hand and manipulation of cards were already well developed in the sixteenth century. With reference to this, see the report by Gerolamo Cardano [50, pages 132-134], perhaps the most skilled gambler of his day, in which there are stories of the miraculous skill and tricks of Dalmagus (or Dalmautus) and of Francesco Soma.

One method of detection—listening to the sound of the cards being dealt—is generally useless in the usual noisy casino atmosphere. It is based on the fact that the second rubs other cards on both its surfaces when dealt, while the top card rubs only on its lower surface. Thus a deal which includes a second generally sounds something like: swish, swish, scrape (second), swish. Of course these sounds and the difference between them are slight; thus it is generally necessary to have quiet to detect this.

To get a very rough idea of the technique of dealing seconds, place a deck of cards in your left hand as though you were about to deal. Now rearrange the deck as follows. The left-front corner should be nestled in the "elbow" or second joint of your index finger. The tip of this finger should be slightly above the top front edge of the deck (it will keep the third card from being pulled forward by the action of the second). The left-rear corner of the deck should be firmly seated in the palm. The second, third, and fourth fingers should go under the deck and around the right side. Their tips should also be slightly above the top of the deck.

Now, with the thumb, which should be lying comfortably on top of the deck toward the front, pull the top card to the left, say half an inch. This half-an-inch figure is only for illustration. An expert would pull the top card to the left (or *down,* for an important alternate variation) only a very small amount. If your grip is proper, the rest of the deck should have been undisturbed by this motion. The corner of the second card is now exposed. By using your right thumb on that corner much as in ordinary dealing, slide the second forward and to the right. When it is part way out, grasp it with the thumb and forefinger just as in ordinary dealing. At about the same time, with the *left* thumb slide the first card back into its original position. If your grip was proper, only the top and second cards were disturbed during the entire process. Proper height of the tips of the second, third, and fourth fingers will prevent the cards below the second from moving when the second card is pulled out. Thus when the deal of the second is complete, the deck appears normal. This is not an expert technique, but it should give you some idea of how second dealing works.

If you used a deck with borders, you may have noticed that, as the second is dealt, the right border* of the top card

---

* I assume the dealer is right-handed throughout the book. If the dealer is left-handed, the words "right" and "left" should be interchanged by the reader throughout many of these discussions.

is almost stationary. However, if a top card is dealt, the right border of the second is partially or totally concealed until the top card has cleared the deck. Thus one way to spot a second being dealt from a deck with borders is to stare from above the deck at the right border (left border from the player's side of the table)) to see whether or not that border moves much as the card is dealt.

To counter this, many second dealers use decks without borders. However, so do a number of honest casinos; thus the mere use of a borderless deck by no means indicates cheating. To make it still harder for the player to see a second being dealt, the dealer generally tips up the front of the deck slightly so that the player views the cards edge on! In this instance the presence or absence of borders is immaterial since the backs of the cards are totally invisible at the instant a card is dealt.

Dealers often tilt the forward end of the deck so far up and back toward their chests that kibitzers who are standing cannot see the back of the top card. In this position anyone can deal a second without being caught. If you try this yourself, simply slide the top card *down* a short distance, deal the second by pulling it forward and up, and restore the top card to its initial position.

Perhaps the most popular type of borderless cards now in use in the casinos are the famous Bee No. 67. The pattern on the backs consists of solid diamonds separated by broken diagonal white stripes. This pattern seems to dazzle or blind the untrained eye; its use seems to increase the difficulties in detecting seconds. When the wrist flick is employed this pattern is even more effective in blinding the eye to the dealing of a second.

Deck Stacking: The High-Low Pickup

During my exploration of casinos to study the cheating methods actually employed, I came across a novel sort of game. The rules were pretty standard except that the game was played with four decks all shuffled together. Further, the cards were dealt from a "shoe." This was a black plastic box that was open at the top. The four decks were shuffled and then placed in the box with their long edges down. There was a slit in the end of the box at the bottom and a small oval hole running up from the slit for a short distance. The backs of the cards showed through the oval. The dealer placed his right thumb through the oval, and to deal the cards, he drew them down and out through the slit, one by one.

This seemed like an ideal game with which to use the Ten-count strategy because, with so many cards in play, the fluctuations in favorability from hand to hand (which results from cards played on the previous hand) would be much smaller than in the one-deck game. Thus when large bets were being placed, there would be much less fluctuation up and down in the bet size. Half an hour's play at the table, waiting for favorable situations, confirmed this. When a run of favorable situations finally came, I changed from a waiting bet of $1 to the $5 to $25 range. There now was a long steady run of favorable situations before the four decks finally ran out. I won about $80. During the next two or three hours of play there were comparable runs with similar results. Altogether, I accumulated about $160. A card-expert friend who was standing by thought the game was so safe that he wandered away. We were soon to get an expensive education.

Shortly afterward, a dealer against whom I had not previously played came to my table. After a few minutes the four decks became favorable. Only this time, I lost nearly every hand. Before the run ended I had lost $250. Startled and suspicious, I then watched the dealer intently.

It was conceivable that he could deal seconds out of the shoe. But how could he identify the top card? Peeking seemed impossible; hence shiners were ruled out. What about marked cards? I watched the dealer's eyes, but he never glanced at the part of the back of the card which was exposed in the oval hole.

The four decks were about average during the next ten runs so I dropped back to $1 waiting bets. However, I was losing on nearly every hand! I then began to count, and in 26 hands, I lost 24, tied one, and won one! The odds against losing at least 24 of 26 hands by chance alone are about 2,000,000 to 1!* I could not believe it. Could I be so tired that I could not count? To be safe I counted the next group of wins and losses by putting chips in little piles. I also was obvious about it so that the dealer would be sure to notice. I wanted to see whether he would alter his behavior. He did not. On the next 14 hands I lost 12, tied one, and won one. The odds against losing at least 36 out of 40 hands by chance alone are about 250,000,000 to one! I was baffled—how did he do it?

And then I noticed an odd thing. The dealer, in picking up his winning pair of Tens, slipped a small card from my hand between them. An accident? I soon found that the used cards were being stacked "low-high, low-high." Then I watched them come out on the deal. Six of us picked up our hands and we all had (*10,3*), (*10,2*), (*10,6*), (*9,5*), etc. I quit playing now and watched the fellow ply his trade. He picked up the cards so smoothly that his interlacing of high and low was almost unnoticeable. He preserved the order of the cards through the shuffle (a false shuffle that looks like a real shuffle but does not affect the cards is standard equipment with card sharps). When he dealt, he never needed to peek or use marked cards. He knew where the cards were: just where he had stacked them.

* Readers who attempt to calculate this figure by assuming that the probabilities of winning and losing are each about 0.5 will get a figure of a little over 200,000 to 1. However, the probability of a tie is nearly 0.1 and should be taken into account. When this is done and we ask, What is the chance of at least 24 losses in 26 hands? with the probability of each loss about 0.45 and the probability of each nonloss (equals tie or win) about 0.55, we get the figure of 2,000,000 to 1.

The casino had dealt with my earlier run of "luck" rather promptly and brutally. I decided to find out whether this was casino policy. I observed that this dealer generally played at the table that was getting the most action. Further, most of the other dealers were less skilled. It seemed likely that they were not "in the know." Sure enough, when I made $1 bets at their tables I was not cheated, and the deck stacker busied himself elsewhere. I struck up conversations with a number of these dealers to check my speculations. I asked whether there had been any winners lately. A few dealers remembered only one such person in the last week (the others remembered none). This person was supposed to have made $500. I guessed that he must have played only a short time and bet fairly large. Sure enough, the dealers said he bet $25 and $50 ($100 on doubling down and pair splitting) and played only a short time. Thus his win corresponded to $20 betting $1 to $2: he was lucky and besides he probably quit before the big guns could reach him.

I later found the high-low pickup used in many other casinos. Here is a test that will give you an idea of the power of the high-low pickup. Let Aces, *10*'s, and *9*'s be high. Let 2 through 7 be low. Let two *8*'s be high and two be low. Stack the deck low-high, low-high. Now deal hands to an imaginary player and to yourself as dealer. Deal so that the player gets low-low and you get high-high. If the order of the deck is low-high, this is automatic. If it is high-low, you can deal seconds. You should win virtually every hand. When a stacked deck is used, get out of that game immediately.

Deck Stacking: The Seven-Card Step-up

One afternoon I was playing head on and betting from $10 to $100. After I had played three or four decks, I noticed that the dealer had started each deck with two hands, one of which was 21 and the other 20. More amazing, his 21 was composed each time of the Ace of Spades and the same Ten-value card, the Queen of Clubs. At my elbow, *employed in a private capacity,* was Mr. Michael MacDougall, one of the world's outstanding detectors of card cheats and a special investigator for the Nevada Gaming Control Board.* (The rest of this chapter is drawn from our experiences on a trip which followed by nine months the trip described in Chapter 5. We spent twelve hours a day for eight days playing dozens of the principal Nevada casinos.) Mr. MacDougall told me that the dealer had set up a card sequence of *7,8,9,10,10,J,Q,K,A.* The sequence was preserved during the shuffle. It is a standard technique of card cheats to shuffle a deck repeatedly in such a way that some preselected clump of cards is left undisturbed. The sequence was "bridged," meaning that it was bent lengthwise down the center, so that when placed face down on a table, the center did not touch the table.

The dealer had left the sequence near the middle of the deck when he offered it to me to cut. An unaware player will generally cut the deck so that the bridged cards become the top cards. Try it yourself and see.

Let us return to our story. After I had cut the *7* to the top, the cards dealt were: *8* to me, *9* to the dealer, *10* to me, *10* to the dealer. He held 19, I held 18. On the next hand the cards went *J* to me, *Q* to the dealer, *K* to me, *A* to the dealer. His natural beat my twenty.

As he picked up these cards he stacked them back into the same sequence. With the next deck the situation repeated itself. The reader can easily convince himself that the same card stack is effective against two or three players.

At this particular casino when the dealers went off duty they put the decks in their pockets. When the new

---

* MacDougall wrote about the cheating we encountered in his syndicated column [35, 37]. He mentioned it on "Open End" when we appeared as guests on April 7, 1963. He exposes cheating in speeches to clubs, dinner groups, and the like, throughout the country. By a strange coincidence, in Nevada he doesn't seem to be in such great demand as an investigator any more.

dealers came on, they took decks out of their pockets. We found out that they were going off and setting the "step-up" into the deck.

It is said that a dealer in Newport, Kentucky, was the inventor of this step-up and that he was so proud of his achievement that he considered demanding royalties from the casinos using it.

A closely related and much more innocent-appearing stacking idea (not currently fashionable) is to let the deck begin each time with a sequence of Tens. Then everyone holds 20 and ties the dealer on the first round. However, succeeding rounds are played from a Ten-poor deck. The effect is the same as if several Tens were removed from the deck before play.

The shuffling technique used to preserve the step-up can be used to convince an onlooker that the deck is not being false-shuffled. The dealer can even square it up after each shuffle. A high-low sequence of considerable length can be preserved this way.

One greedy blond dealer against whom I played briefly was preserving a high-low clump *twenty* cards long. When I called her attention to the clump, she refused to shuffle to destroy it.

Often one sees a blackjack table standing empty, attended by a dealer and awaiting customers. It is common practice at such tables to leave the deck spread out face up. Presumably this is so the player will see that all the cards are there. If the deck is newly opened and the cards are in their original order, it is easily possible to tell whether or not any cards are missing. It is not easy to tell this when the cards have been mixed up. And as soon as you sit down the deck is scooped up, shuffled, and brought into play; therefore you have no time to check the deck. Mr. Michael MacDougall observed that if we stood back from such an empty table and examined the deck we could find the step-ups all laid out and waiting. We went to a suspect casino. At the first table we approached, we saw the step-up. We bet $1. The dealer offered us the deck to cut, without even bothering to shuffle. As expected, we cut the step-up to the top and the dealer received 20, followed by 21. We commented on how we had been cheated by a step-up and the dealer laughed happily, proud of his handiwork and proud that someone finally appreciated it [37].

Anchor Men

One large hotel on the Las Vegas strip seemed to be completely free from cheating. After I had won a couple of hundred dollars in half an hour, playing $5 to $50, one of the pit bosses jokingly asked how the system was working. MacDougall told him "up and down, like an elevator." Since the pit boss was friendly enough and we were running out of places in which to play, we adopted the following policy with this hotel. Bet $5 to $50 and stop playing after we had won $200 or played forty-five minutes, whichever was sooner. Forty-five minutes was short enough so that in a few minutes I could fully recover from the strains of counting, refreshed and relaxed. If we stopped at $200, our win was small enough, compared to ordinary chance fluctuations, to seem to be just a little luck.

(The reader may be puzzled at the contrast between this timid low-scale betting and the earlier test reported in Chapter 5. Conditions in Nevada seemed to have changed drastically between these two times. On this trip we learned that if we won more than $250 to $500 or placed a single bet above $50 to $100, we did so at our peril.)

This casino welcomed us back the next few times we came. We proceeded to beat them eight times in a row. We were busily at work on a ninth win when the pit boss called over our dealer and told him something. My friend Mr. MacDougall overheard the dealer say, "All right, I'll give it to him." When the dealer returned we asked him what he was going to give me. He only smiled. Our eyes locked onto the dealer's hands and eyes. He did not do anything suspicious. Puzzled, we watched and played. In a few minutes an individual who would have otherwise seemed inconspicuous came steaming down the aisle behind our row of blackjack tables. He was passing our table at high speed when the pit boss whistled. He made a sharp turn on his heel and plunked down in the seat to my right. I cut my bets and awaited developments.

We immediately noticed that the dealer now might be peeking, but he did not deal any seconds. The new player watched the dealer's eyes before he decided whether to draw or stand. I tried to see his cards when the bets were being settled in order to tell if he was following a consistent strategy. But either he threw his cards in face down or the dealer picked them up so that I saw only their backs. Finally, I got two glances at this fellow's cards.

He stood on hard 8 once and drew on hard 19 the second time! Further scrutiny confirmed the fact that the dealer was peeking. If he wanted me to get the top card, he signaled the new player (termed an "anchor man") to stand. If he wanted to keep the top card from me (for example, suppose I doubled down and he saw it was a Nine or Ten), he signaled the anchor man to draw. An anchor man makes the dealing of seconds unnecessary. With marked cards even the peek would become unnecessary.

The dealer could easily infer from my behavior, formed through long habit, whether I was going to double down, draw, stand, or split a pair. It is thus a useful art in casino blackjack to be able to play with a poker face. An easier way to combat an anchor man is to wait until your turn to even look at your cards. In this way, you cannot possibly help the dealer who uses an anchor man.

We moved to another table, the one farthest from where we were. I sat so that a player already at that table was on my right, occupying the anchor man's future seat.

The word was passed to the dealer and the anchor man waited patiently. In a few minutes the player on my right got up and the anchor man plopped down. We left. The fun was over in that casino [35].

Alternatively, the anchor man may be seated on the dealer's right. He then stands or draws according to signals from the dealer. This enables the dealer, whose turn is next, to draw more desirable cards for himself. The entire table loses to the dealer's superior cards, in contrast to the first use of the anchor man, in which only one player seems singled out for hard luck.

We had several additional incidents with anchor men in other casinos. They suggest to me that Nevada, a state without seacoast, has the biggest "navy" of any state in the union.

The Gratuitous Peek

When the dealer has a Ten up, he immediately checks his hole card to see whether he has a natural. When he has an Ace up, he first asks the players if they want insurance (assuming the insurance rule is being used) and only after this is decided does he check his hole card. When he has any other card up, there is no reason for him to check his hole card before his turn to play. I have on a number of occasions seen dealers check their hole card when an Ace was up before they offered the players insurance. They then tried by their actions and manner to influence the player. If they had a natural either they would not offer insurance or they would rush the player. If they had no natural, they gave the player plenty of time and even hinted with their facial expressions that insurance was wise. Once in a while I have seen dealers look at their hole card immediately when they had neither a Ten nor an Ace up. They then continue to peek until they find a card they need, which they hold for themselves by dealing seconds.

Mechanics on Call

A (card) mechanic is a skilled cheat who accomplishes his ends by sleight of hand. Some larger casinos have their own mechanics working as dealers on the regular shifts. Since mechanics are paid much better than ordinary dealers, a casino which cheats will, for reasons of economy, hire only as many as pay for themselves by the extra revenue. Often there is only one mechanic per shift. One morning I was betting $10 to $100 and winning. After a while, the dealer went off duty and his relief came on. Suddenly the pit boss rushed over, scolded the relief, sent him to another table, and made our dealer stay on. A few minutes later another dealer the pit boss had summoned relieved our dealer. The new dealer was, according to the expert who was protecting me, a mechanic. We could not see any definite cheating, only suspicious moves. But good mechanics can often conceal their move from the most skilled eyes, leaving only a few suspicious side effects. We immediately lost nearly every bet. At the $10 level we lost a couple of hundred dollars of our winnings in a few minutes.

We walked across the street to a smaller casino, one Periodically these boxes are brought into the counting $5 to $50, we were well ahead after twenty minutes. The pit boss was grimly hostile. Then he made a phone call. More time passed. Then we looked at our watches and saw that it was time for our dealer to go off duty, yet he was not. In "a city without clocks," always carry a watch to see if your dealers are being changed after what you observe to be the regular length of time for a shift, and at no other time. A break in the pattern indicates trouble.

Our dealer had been on duty thirty-seven minutes (thirty was normal in this casino) when a man dressed in a white shirt and black pants like the other dealers, but without the apron of that casino, hastened through the front door and up to our table. He immediately began to deal. We spotted him as a mechanic. With a smile he purred, "Would you gentlemen like a drink?" The pit boss became relaxed and in good spirits. A wave of friendliness seemed to pervade the grim, barren, midmorning desolation of the place. We left.

Miscellaneous Methods

There are so many ways for the dealer to cheat that we can only give a brief introduction to the subject here. The interested reader can study it in much greater detail in the many references that are available [15, 22, 36, 53, 58, 66]. Many interesting facts were also presented during a Senate investigation of gambling in the fall of 1961 [30, 42].

Despite all our warnings and the frequency with which dealers cheat, there are a number of casinos that are scrupulously honest. Our purpose in this chapter is to make the reader acutely aware of the dangers of cheating and to give him enough knowledge so that, in most cases, he will be able to spot it and change casinos before suffering a serious loss. It should now be evident that it is suicide to play in a place that cheats; you have virtually no hope of winning.

Avoiding the Cheats

As a practical matter, it is not likely that you will be able to actually catch much of the cheating that you meet. The better cheats can only be spotted by experts, and sometimes not even then. How can you avoid serious losses from cheating?

The best method I know of (the paper-route technique described earlier) is now being quite widely and successfully used. Here again is the idea. Divide your stake into ten or twenty equal parts. For example, starting with $200 you might divide it into ten parts of $20 each. When you sit down to play, buy $20 worth of chips. Play until you either lose your $20 or double it. Then quit. If you are still playing after an hour, quit anyhow. Go on to another casino. Return to casinos and dealers you do well against. Avoid those you do poorly against. This way, no one cheat hurts you much. And you never play a cheat twice.

11

Can the Cheating
Be Stopped?

LIFE *Breaks the Cheating Story*

Life magazine ran a feature article about the author and his methods in which *Life*'s staff writer Paul O'Neil broke the long-concealed story of cheating in Nevada blackjack [49]. "Thorp has been victimized by crooked dealers. . . . He has been backed off (thrown out) by pit bosses, he has been harassed by shills, plied endlessly with booze, eyed significantly by plug-uglies and, on two occasions, rendered spectacularly rubber-legged and goggled-eyed by knockout drops, courtesy of the house."*

In preparation for his article, O'Neil read my work. Then he spent a week in Las Cruces studying me and my ideas about blackjack. Next he spent four days with me in Las Vegas (I was there for the 1963 Fall Joint Computer

---

* This was the house's last attempt to stop my five-night winning streak at baccarat. After my team and I pushed our win streak to seven nights, the rules were changed. The side bet we exploited was removed from the layout. See [59, 70] for details.

Conference). He watched me pile up $420 in winnings in the four and a half hours I could spare from my work to play blackjack. (My bets ranged from $1 to $25, depending on circumstances, and averaged about $5.) During the twenty minutes that I was posing for pictures at the Tropicana (unrecognized by the management), the tables kindly rewarded me with $62.50.

The *Life* article was painstakingly accurate and thoroughly researched by O'Neil.

Even the authors of *The Green Felt Jungle* were unsure—probably due to insufficient information—about the cheating situation. The dust jacket of the hardback painted the most sordid picture of the other phases of Nevada gambling and then concluded, "Ironically, the gambling equipment is possibly the only thing in Las Vegas that is really on the level."

Replies from Nevada

The *Life* story could not be ignored. There were cries of protest from out West. For example, Edward A. Olsen, chairman of the Nevada Gaming Control Board in Carson City, wrote in a letter to *Life* [48, p. 27],

Sirs:

Neither your writer nor Dr. Thorp has evidence to substantiate such statements as: "Thorp has been victimized by crooked dealers in almost all of the major casinos in Nevada."

Your writer's statement that Dr. Edward Thorp "usually knows in his nerve ends just when he is being double-crossed" appears more worthy of scientific investigation than his system of counting the cards in a 21 game. I think *Life* has libeled the state of Nevada.

EDWARD A. OLSEN, *Chairman*
State Gaming Control Board

On April 3, shortly after *Life*'s article appeared, Mr. Olsen closed the Silver Slipper, a Las Vegas casino, on charges of cheating. Meanwhile, several casinos have made changes in their blackjack rules to thwart the Thorp system.—ED.

But the right hand evidently did not know what the left was doing. For at about the time the Olsen letter was sent, a Nevada newspaper announced [25]:

STRIP CASINO CLOSED BY STATE. SILVER SLIPPER RAIDED. "CROOKED DICE" CHARGED BY GAMING OFFICIALS.

The story went on to tell how five dice were picked up on a routine check of the crap tables. All five dice were later found to be percentage dice. "The official statement of facts was signed by Control Board Chairman Edward A. Olsen. . . ." An earlier incident of cheating at blackjack was reported as a second charge:

The Silver Slipper had no serious enforcement problems before last year. It appeared then in complaints filed by the Gaming Control Board with the gaming commission after undercover agents found a dealer cheating at 21. The casino's management was notified, and the dealer was fired.

No action was taken at that time, but the incident is now listed as a second cause of action in the current complaint.

How Card Cheating Can Be Stopped

In the first edition I gave a detailed and simple procedure which could be used to stop virtually all the blackjack cheating methods described in this book. These suggestions seem to have fallen on deaf ears in Nevada.

What can be done by private citizens or by the federal

government to eradicate the cheating? Many people have asked me this and I have thought long and hard about the answer.

The great stumbling block is, how can you get evidence that will stand up in court about something so intangible as sleight-of-hand card cheating? What is needed is somehow to get photographs, or better, movies of the cheats in action. Movies would be ideal, for the cheating move could be followed frame by frame. Photos should show the cheating move, the cheat's face (for identification), and the club emblem on the layout.

Discouraging further cheating would then be quite simple. Publish the pictures and an account of the action in a nationally distributed book or magazine.

I am told that the most practical (though still difficult) way of obtaining the pictures would be with a subminiature Japanese video tube and to transmit the pictures by radio to a remotely located recorder. There might be legal difficulties, however. I understand that a Nevada state law prohibits taking pictures inside a casino without the casino's permission.

How the U. S. Treasury Can Recover Tax Money
Lost from Stealing off the Top

In the summer of 1962 I was visited by an undercover agent of the U. S. Treasury Department. He was one of a half-dozen or so such agents who were part of a larger investigation of tax evasion by certain casinos in Nevada. He told me that certain casinos were taking large sums of money "off the top." In blackjack, for example, when you buy chips at the table, your money is generally pushed through a slot in the table into a locked box underneath. Periodically these boxes are brought into the counting rooms where they are opened, and the contents are recorded as part of the casino's gross income. According to this agent, a common practice is to list the contents on an adding-machine tape, recording the number of hundreds, fifties, twenties, and change.

He asserted that some casinos keep two adding-machine tapes, one with the true figures and the other with greatly reduced figures. The smaller figures are reported to the government. The difference between the true gross and the reported gross escapes taxes.

I asked the agent how he knew about all this. He said that he and other undercover agents were posing as big spenders and gambling conspicuously. They were able to ingratiate themselves enough to be taken to the counting rooms as part of a guided tour.

He said that the experiences of the agents suggested that about one third of the winnings was being taken off the top at that time. If the gross declared casino gambling income in Nevada was $220,000,000 for 1961 and if $180,000,000 went for expenses, the taxes would be about $10,000,000 on the $40,000,000 net, leaving a profit of about $30,000,000. But a suspected $110,000,000 more was being taken off the top. This would mean a true profit of $140,000,000! Taxes escaping the government would exceed $25,000,000.

The agent had to come to see me for two reasons. First, he and the others had learned to play my winning system and how to spot cheating. The government "couldn't afford" to have them lose huge sums at the tables just to get tours of the counting rooms. He wanted additional pointers.

Second, the agent wondered whether there was a way of proving, statistically perhaps, that the theft of money off the top was taking place. We conferred for a couple of days, after which I suggested the following scheme. Here is the original text (except for minor changes and clarifications, mostly indicated by brackets) of my suggestion to the federal government.

Operation "Money-Pump"

June, 1962

INTRODUCTION. There is strong reason to believe that the Nevada casinos, when counting the "drop" from the gaming tables (i.e., the money that accumulates in the money boxes under the tables between collections), take money "off the top." This means that in the counting rooms they set aside money from the total so that the reported gross total is less than the true total. The evidence is of two kinds. First, an agent of the federal government has several times been an eyewitness to this in casino counting rooms. Secondly, the casinos expend vast sums which are not covered by entries in their books, for items like complimentary girls for customers, mechanics who cheat the customers at the tables (they get a fraction of the take and a higher daily wage; I've talked at length with one of them) and perhaps for the financing of nation-wide rackets. Where does this [extra] money [that the casinos spend but don't report] come from? Logic suggests it comes "off the top" of the [casino] operation it is being used to support.

In 1961 the Nevada casino gross gambling revenue was around $221,000,000 and a net taxable income of around $40,000,000 was reported. If the casinos are taking a mere one sixth off the top, they have a hidden additional potentially taxable income of $44,000,000 and are more than doubling their supposed net income (the reported $40,000,000 taxes down to about $30,000,000)! On the basis of the evidence cited earlier, it seems likely that the amounts taken off considerably exceed one sixth of the total.

There was a famous muckraker, Lincoln Steffens, who in the period 1900-1910 exposed in a sensational series of magazine articles the then emerging pattern of corruption in our big cities and in state governments. In his autobiography he summarized his experiences in a maxim: "Wherever a graft exists for the taking, people will arise to take it." The casinos can take money off the top with impunity: no preventive machinery now exists! Further, if a certain casino is taking off, say, a hundred thousand, why not take off a million instead? Since if by some accident they're caught the penalties are the same, why not take off all the traffic will bear?

We propose a test which will either clear the casinos of this charge, or will produce court evidence of such strength that the responsible casino bigwigs can be convicted in criminal court. On this latter event, which seems likely for some of the casinos, the effect of a few convictions should lead the remaining offenders in the casino set to the "path of righteousness." The potential gain in income tax should each year pay for the project scores of times over!

THE PLAN. We propose to gamble at selected tables of selected casinos. We would buy chips with hundred-dollar bills whose serial numbers will have been pre-recorded (this record is not essential to our main object but does have an additional application that will be discussed in a later report). We would play continuously from one collection to another, recording the total number of hundred-dollar bills that go into the money box and noting the number which were ours. A current practice is for the casino to record the number of bills of various denominations and to label the record with the table and shift number. Thus, at the end of the casino tax year, certain of the records can be checked to see if money was taken off the top or not. Our evidence is that it is currently taken in the form of hundred-dollar bills, in a proportion that increases as the number of hundred-dollar bills increases. Thus our test is specific for the problem.

Now, it is widely believed that the casinos necessarily have a certain percentage advantage over the player at each of the games. At blackjack, for example, a typical player seems to lose in the long run from 3 to 5 per cent of the total amount of his bets. Of course, he usually rebets his money several times. Thus he generally loses several times this percentage of his original bankroll. This is measured by the casino when it determines how much of the drop it "holds," i.e., what fraction of the amount the player invests in chips is won by the casino. In blackjack it is estimated that the casino holds 20 to 30 per cent of the drop, i.e., the player loses from his investment an amount equal to from about four to ten times the casino's edge over him. This is due, as we've mentioned before, to the fact that he generally rebets his money several times and thus the house extracts its percentage several times over.

It might seem from this that to pump $120,000 into several blackjack tables (perhaps $5,000 per table per shift would be adequate, thus allowing 60 samples), some $30,000 of playing capital would be required and consumed. However, it has been proven (both in theory and at the gaming tables) [67,68,69] that there is a *winning* (!) strategy for the player at blackjack. This makes it possible to pump in really large amounts of money—in the millions if desired— with the aid of the same $30,000 bankroll. We propose a $30,000 bankroll for playing capital. The hundreds of samples thus attainable offer statistical and legal advantages over the smaller number of 60.

We propose that a team of perhaps twelve agents, some male and some female, learn this strategy (two or three days training is sufficient!) and systematically but as inconspicuously as possible pump in very large sums in various casinos. At the end of a tax year many hundreds of table-shift record cards could then be checked to see if money was taken off the top. With such a sample size, if the money were being taken it would certainly show up. Further, since the people who count also sign the record cards and have been there since the money box was unlocked, they are absolutely liable for taking money off the top. Now the evidence would probably be stronger from the standpoint of convincing a jury if the same individuals were found guilty of several violations rather than only one. Our sample size is designed to make this [more] likely.

As far as I know, "Operation Moneypump" is filed away in a dusty Federal drawer, certain casinos are still taking money off the top, and our national tax collection still doesn't cover our expenditures.

12

Science Versus Chance

The appearance of numerous system players will ultimately necessitate important changes in the game of twenty-one as it is now played. We can gain some first insights into these changes by discussing the means through which the Nevada casinos have dealt with the handful of successful players (whom we refer to as "count" players because they counted cards) that has appeared in that state during the last decade. Most of the stories surrounding these early players are not a matter of public record or even known beyond a small circle of acquaintances. No part of the legend became known to me until sometime after I had completed the winning strategy outlined in this book and had arrived in Nevada to test it in actual play.

Early Winning Players

The first of the successful system players, a much different personality from the others in the group and in no way representative, was a colorful individual known as

"Greasy John." Large and obese, he acquired his name from his habit of coming to the casino with a large bag of very greasy fried chicken. He played for as long as twenty hours at a stretch, never leaving the table. The casino supplied the drinks, and innumerable meals of varying sizes could always be drawn from the huge bag of chicken. It soon became apparent that "Greasy John" wanted to play alone. As crowded as the casinos are, once he became a familiar face he did not have much trouble keeping other players away. His profanity and drinking drove off all but the hardiest of women players and finally the casinos forbade all women to play at the same table with him.

Since Greasy John's hands were generally dripping with chicken fat, the cards soon became too oily to handle comfortably. Even though decks were changed frequently, the grease was sufficient to drive away the men players.

Greasy John played for long hours day after day, and in a few months he became wealthy enough to retire. He suffered a heart attack and died shortly afterwards. We have no knowledge of the system that Greasy John used. It seems probable from surviving details that he employed end play. As noted in an earlier chapter, end play will produce astronomical gains in a short time in spite of the fact that the player's basic playing strategy is poor. Furthermore, end play is a very natural idea, easy to verify empirically, and it probably has occurred to a great many players.

For those players who follow "System Smitty," we have in most cases omitted the details of the colorful backgrounds of the individuals involved, and the parts of their adventures that might serve to identify them. We also have regretfully omitted the human-interest portions of the legend, involving areas such as sex, vice, "con men," and the mob. We must further emphasize that the legend is a composite of many separate stories told to me by different people. However, for the most part the stories are mutually consistent and the people who told them were direct participants. Therefore, I believe the story is substantially accurate.

To my knowledge, the first person who employed a "count" system in successful casino play was Benjamin F. ("System Smitty") Smith, a well-known figure in the Las Vegas casinos [1]. According to Mr. Z, a mutual acquaintance who has seen Smitty's voluminous notebooks, Smitty spent several years playing out 100,000 hands in an effort to determine the proper standing numbers when a Ten-count was employed. The system, as described to me by Mr. Z, gave a fair approximation of the totals to stand on for various values of the ratio Tens/others. However there were certain moderate errors, which resulted, at least partly, from the nature of the system.

In addition to the moderate errors in standing numbers that were part of System Smitty's method, there was no detailed strategy for doubling down and pair splitting. These factors, in toto, probably cut 2 or 3 per cent off the player's advantage, not to mention the increased rate of attrition of the small "waiting" bets. Since the bulk of the favorable bets are in the 0 to 3 per cent range, the player's rate of win is greatly diminished. The only alternative for the player who wants to make a big win is to overbet his capital (in terms of the theory of proportional or "fixed fraction" betting [23,70,76]), greatly increasing the chance of ruin, and hope for the best.

Smitty probably did precisely this, for he has had many spectacular win-loss sequences. Mr. Z said he was present one night when Smitty won $108,000 at the blackjack tables (that is a considerable sum with a $500 limit) and lost it all back by the next morning. He did not even have the price of breakfast left.

Smitty's system, which was first used in the mid-fifties, I believe, seems to have spread to a small group of players including a certain old-time gambler whom we shall call

Mr. F, Mr. F's mistress, the Mr. X of Chapter 5, Mr. Z, the little dark-haired guy mentioned previously, and a young player commonly known both as Junior and as "Sonny."

This group of players pumped large sums of money out of the blackjack tables within the next few years. There is no way to determine exactly how large the sums were. For what it is worth, the "grapevine" credits Mr. F with $50,000 gross winnings, Mr. Z with $56,000 gross (afterwards divided with his bankrollers), and Mr. X with $100,000 to $150,000 gross. The little dark-haired guy is supposed to have cleared $250,000.

In any case, the members of the group won large amounts in short times in only a few casinos, and as a consequence the casinos, which had initially been skeptical of the possibility that the game could be beaten, finally barred each of the members of the group from play at the twenty-one tables and spread the warning.

Casino Countermeasures Against Count Players

During and after this period a number of casino responses and countermeasures to count players either came into existence or developed further.

Cheating. Cheating has already been discussed.

Barring. A casino can exclude a small class of players without difficulty. However, this solution does not seem feasible on a large scale. With the early system players, photographs could be distributed to all local casinos, but for thousands of players this idea is simply impractical. Along these same lines, even though a given casino's employees may remember a particular individual and bar him from further play, barring is not a defense for the casinos as a whole because it is possible that the individual may work his way through the hundreds of existing casinos and allay suspicion by winning only a few hundred dollars at each one.

It is obvious that casino employees are trained to re-member people. Junior (also called "Sonny") told me that after he was universally barred in the casinos, he went to the make-up department of one of the Hollywood movie studios. He paid $500 for a complete disguise. On the basis of his facial structure, color, and build they decided to dis-guise him as middle-aged Chinese. The disguise even in-cluded a carapace to be fitted over his torso. He tried out his nice new outfit one evening in a casino in which there were six employees on duty who knew him. Five of them paid no attention to him. Shortly after he began to play, the sixth employee wandered over from the bar, spotted him at once, and exclaimed, "Hey, look everybody. There's Sonny all dressed up like a Chinese." Junior still keeps his beloved Chinese outfit stored away somewhere, buried under years of accumulated dust.

Shuffle up. Shuffle up is another casino strategy that is effective against a small class of players but has a serious drawback when system players become numerous. It costs the casinos money by slowing down the game, and it also alienates some customers. Further, as we have already pointed out in Chapter 9, shuffle up is fraught with diffi-culties for the casino. How does a dealer know when he is facing a system player and when he is not? The best count players can play faster than any dealer can deal, and smoother and more effortlessly than most players. Thus they have ample freedom to adopt a guise. And there are many subtle ways to camouflage varying one's bet size (when nec-essary the variation can be made quite small, 2 to 1 or even less).

Further Developments

As we noted in Chapter 9, the casinos tried rules changes and gave them up. The outcome of the experiments with automatic blackjack machines remains to be seen.

On the player's side there have been several new developments. In the first edition we pointed out that low-cost miniature devices could be manufactured which would do most of the work of counting cards and playing the various strategies.

Such a device, called the Beat the Dealer Computer,* was designed by Dr. Tom Bean with the assistance of the author. It is a palm-sized plastic device much like a circular slide rule. The player turns tiny dials when he sees cards. This particular device plays the Ten-count strategy for one deck. One dial counts Tens and the other counts non-Tens. The ratio and the player's advantage can be read off at any time. Recommended bet sizes are also indicated.

The computer can be used as an aid in learning the Ten-count system. Players who wish to use it also in the casinos can hold the computer in their palm and operate it by "touch." Tiny bumps indicating the bet size and ratio can be felt. The dials, designed to click off one card at a time, can be operated without being looked at.

For those who learn better by ear than by eye, a long-playing phonograph record that teaches the point-count strategy is available.** The record which I wrote and narrate, is a complete, self-contained course in winning blackjack. It also covers casino countermeasures, camouflage, tactics, and recent developments.

Computers Versus Casinos

The ultimate player would be a high-speed computer. A first step in this direction was taken several years ago by Robert Bamford of Jet Propulsion Laboratory. Bamford designed a "black box" to play blackjack. It is an electric analog device that performs an approximate computation for an arbitrary subset of cards. It tells the player his approximate correct strategy and approximate advantage.

* The computer and information about it can be obtained by writing Beat the Dealer Co., Box 635, Alamogordo, New Mexico.
** It is distributed by Scientific Research Records, Inc., Box 63, Palm Springs, California, for $1.95 plus 25¢ postage.

Cards are read in by turning knobs attached to gang-switches. Information output is from a meter that is interrogated by push buttons. The analog calculation is based on a matrix approach similar in spirit to the matrix formulation of the infinite-deck baccarat calculations of [70]. The device I saw consisted of two portable-radio-sized boxes wired together. Miniaturization to book-size or smaller would be quite feasible. The device could be linked to the player by radio. It could instruct him automatically upon interrogation.

Bamford tried to persuade two casinos to play his machine, but, in a comedy of double-talk and evasion reported by the *Pasadena Star-News,* the casinos frustrated his test.

But a match between another computer and a casino did take place. At the time of the 1963 Western Joint Computer Conference, a trio of Los Angeles computermen took on the Tropicana Hotel. The three operated the eight pound LGP-21 for an hour. The machine's method of play was inspired by the ideas of the first edition of *Beat the Dealer.*

In a one-hour match, witnessed by Paul O'Neil of *Life,* myself, and many others, the machine won $360 [44]. Bets varied from $2 to $42. And the machine won in spite of the fact that the harried computermen made several costly errors.

The next step is obvious. A computer can be instructed quite easily always to make the best possible play. The player simply tells the machine what the casino rules are and then informs it of the cards he has seen and of the shuffles. Then, a split second after the player tells the machine his cards, it would tell the player the best play.

It is technically feasible to link a casino blackjack player by radio to a remotely located giant machine which does the actual playing. The player would win at several times the rate of the best human players. Furthermore, special situations such as the Puerto Rican end play of Chapter 6 could be exploited easily and precisely.

If a large computer were used, it could play several games at once. In industry computers are now commonly used on such a time-sharing basis: while the machine is waiting for more information on one problem, it spends its precious time solving another.

Science Versus Chance

The mathematical theory of probability originated in the sixteenth and seventeenth centuries with the consideration by Cardano, Pascal, and others of various gambling games, and with their investigations as to whether or not there were systems for beating them. Most notably, these games were the forerunners and relatives of craps. From that time until the recent past, a series of persons whose names are illustrious in mathematics and physics have thought seriously about gambling games (and have often made important related contributions to the mathematical theory of probability!). In addition to Cardano and Pascal, some earlier examples are Fermat, James and Daniel Bernouilli, Laplace, and Poisson.

At the turn of this century, the great mathematician and physicist Henri Poincaré considered the possibility of predicting the outcome of a trial of roulette by physical rather than mathematical methods. He concluded that this was impossible via an argument based on the mathematical concept of a continuous function. However, the concepts involved illustrated certain philosophical concepts in science (see [52], pages 69-70 and pages 76-77). Also early in this century the great English statistician Karl Pearson spent many years analyzing the records of certain roulette wheels. However, for more than forty years there seem to have been no successful scientific attempts to devise winning gambling systems.

The modern high-speed computer, essential to a care-

ful analysis of blackjack, has been widely available for only
the last ten or fifteen years; without such a computer the
analysis on which this book is based would have been impossible.* With the continuing rapid growth in the number
of scientists and engineers, and the rise of fantastic new
scientific tools, the interest in the possibility of winning
gambling systems is increasing.

In the first edition we predicted that scientifically based
winning systems for other games would appear. Within a
few months of publication, a team of trained players and I
went to Nevada with a winning system for the baccarat
side bets [59,70].

We averaged $100 an hour for seven nights in casino
number one. It cried uncle and barred us. Later it removed
the side bet. At casino number two we upped the bets. We
averaged $1,000 an hour for two hours and they barred us.
The side bets then disappeared in Nevada.**

Allan Wilson gives an interesting and entertaining account of attempts to identify and beat defective ("biased")
roulette wheels in [80]. There are also several people (including myself) who possess a method for beating roulette
wheels whether or not they are defective!

I played roulette on a regulation wheel in the base-
ment lab of a world-famous scientist. We used the method
and steadily averaged 44 per cent profit. In an hour's run,
betting no more than $25 per number, we won a fictional
$8,000! There are certain electronic problems which have
so far kept the method from being used on a large scale in
the casinos. (The few times I have used it to turn two or
three dimes suddenly into a pile of silver dollars has
caused enormous excitement.)

* The IBM 704 high-speed computer which we used spent about
three hours calculating. It calculates many millions of times as fast as
a human and is nearly error-free. It would have taken roughly ten
thousand man-years to do the same calculations with the aid of a desk
calculator. Still bigger and faster machines are now available.
** As this is written, the Carousel in Las Vegas is trying a modified
and "safer" version of these side bets.

The method works, and the story behind its discovery and development is a long and fascinating one. It will be even more fascinating when, sometime in the next few years, some of the few who possess the idea cash in on it in the casinos.

The game of poker has perhaps received more intense mathematical study than any other game. With the extensive theoretical research that has already been done on the game, it should be possible to construct a practical playing strategy superior to that currently used by any expert.

The Stock Market

The greatest gambling game on earth is the one played daily through the brokerage houses across the country. The customers bet $250,000,000 or so each trading day. A year's action exceeds $60,000,000,000. The advantage of this gambling game are two. First, it presumably serves a social purpose by helping to finance companies (when stock issues are first sold on the market). Second, the average "value" of stocks has tended strongly upward over the last century so that the game has an "advantage," on "average," for the player.*

The similarity between the casinos and the brokerage houses is striking. The customers' men are the croupiers. The commissions correspond to the house percentage. The board rooms are the casinos themselves. The stock exchanges and the ticker tape are the gambling devices. The superstitions, unfounded slogans, and sayings of Wall Street correspond to those of the gamblers': "The dice are hot."

To a good first approximation, stocks show the same mathematical characteristics of randomness that are shown by the chance devices in the gaming houses [7]. But a number of patterns are now being discovered. To convince

---

* Quotes are used extensively here to indicate that I am using familiar words with well-defined meanings to roughly indicate other ideas. Precise explanations of these other ideas, to which I have given much thought, are too complex and lengthy for me to discuss them here.

yourself that there are patterns in stock prices, pick up tomorrow morning's newspaper. (I assure you I haven't seen it yet.) Notice that the stock prices are given as a whole number followed by a fraction, for example 23⅛. Now run down the page and tally the number of each ending that occurs. You will find whole numbers will be most common, then halves, then quarters. The lowly eighths occur least often. (I ignore sixteenths.) In addition to this pattern of endings exhibited by the market as a whole, each stock has its own characteristic pattern for these fractional endings.

The mathematical analysis of the stock market is being undertaken by many groups. With the advance in computer technology and mathematical theory, we can expect dramatic progress in predicting stock prices. (Unfortunately this is not the place to detail the results now being obtained by myself and others.)

The Future

In the last part of the twentieth century there will be many new applications of scientific and particularly mathematical methods to the prediction of phenomena heretofore called "chance." We have tried to indicate a few of the developments that are similar in spirit to those described in this book. But most of the possibilities are beyond the reach of our present imagination and dreams. It will be exciting to see them unfold.

Addendum

Blackjack in England

The winning systems described in this book appear to apply with full power to blackjack as played in England. The following detailed discussion suggests that the methods that succeeded in Las Vegas and Puerto Rico should do equally well here. The discussion will be of interest to English readers and to those who travel in England. It will also be of general interest to readers who wish to check their understanding of Table 9.2 and its use in analyzing casinos' rules variations. The computations made from Table 9.2 may differ slightly from the results in this addendum, because I introduced extra refinements whenever I was aware of them.

The following is a description of the rules and customs of three big London gambling clubs, sent in by an English reader, followed by my analysis and comments. The rules and customs are those given as "typical" in Chapter 2, with the exceptions noted below.

In each case there are from one to six players besides

the dealer, and four decks are used, dealt from a shoe. (Four decks are disadvantageous to the player.)

Casino 1

RULES. (*a*) No card is burned.

(*b*) The minimum bet is £1 and the maximum is £50.

(*c*) All cards are dealt face up, except for one of the dealer's cards. (This is a considerable aid in card counting.)

(*d*) A player who splits a pair and receives a third card of the same value is permitted to split again. (This increases the player's advantage.)

(*e*) The insurance bet may be up to the *whole* amount of the player's original bet, not merely half the value. (This is very favorable to the system player. When insurance is advantageous, the card-counting player should always insure for the whole amount.

Customs. The dealer always deals down to and including the last card. (This is extremely favorable for the card counter. Also, end play can be used to tremendous advantage here. No casino can long continue to play head on against an expert player with this rule in effect.)

Conclusions. The basic-strategy player has a disadvantage of 0.27%. An average or better system player will win at more than the typical rate (assuming he takes some advantage of end play).

Casino 2

RULES. (*a*) See 1(a).

(*b*) The minimum is 5s. and the maximum is £50.

(*c*) See 1(d).

(*d*) A player who splits a pair is not permitted to

double down on the new hands. (This decreases the player's advantage.)

(e) Doubling down is only permitted on totals of hard 9, 10, and 11, and soft 19, 20, and 21. (This decreases the player's advantage.)

(f) A player who doubles down on 9 and gets a 2 may draw another card. (This increases the player's advantage. A correct strategy calls for slightly more frequent doubling down on 9, but this refinement can be ignored.)

Customs. See Casino 1.

Conclusions. The basic-strategy player has a disadvantage of about 0.60%. An average or better system player will win at about the typical rate (assuming he takes some advantage of end play.)

Casino 3

RULES. (a) The minimum bet is 10s. and the maximum is £50.

(b) The cards are all dealt face up. The dealer does not get his second card until the players have taken such additional cards as they require. A player who increases his stake by splitting and/or doubling down loses his increased stake if the dealer gets a natural. (This is somewhat unfavorable to the player. When the dealer shows an Ace or Ten, be much more conservative about doubling down or splitting pairs.)

(c) If the dealer has soft 17, he may draw or not, as he likes, after looking at the players' cards. (This is quite unfavorable to the player, for the dealer can see what they have and so make decisions quite favorable to himself. His precise gain is not known.)

(d) A player who splits Aces and obtains a third

Ace may split again, but he may not split further. (This is favorable to the player.)

(e) If a player splits a pair of 10-value cards and draws an Ace to one of the split hands, it counts as a natural. But a 10-value card drawn to a split Ace counts merely as 21. (This variation is favorable to the player. Tens should tend to be split slightly more than normally.)

(f) See 2(e).

(g) See 1(e).

Customs. The dealer shuffles about twenty cards before the end of the shoe. (Not serious, in my experience.) At one time this casino allowed doubling down, with the above totals, on any number of cards. A player whose total after doubling down was hard 10 or 11 or soft 20 or 21 was allowed to redouble and receive a fourth card. Also, the dealer dealt down to the last card.

Conclusions. The basic-strategy player would appear to be at a disadvantage of roughly 0.61% or more. A system player will win, but at perhaps half or less of the typical rate.

In this way readers may analyze any casino with the aid of Table 9.2.

APPENDIX

Basic Probabilities for the Complete Deck

An understanding of this appendix is not essential to the rest of the book. It is included for the interest of mathematically inclined readers.

The tables in this appendix are an extract of the computer's results for the case in which cards are dealt from one complete deck. Results like these, including one full set for each of the decks described in Table 4.1, were used to construct the blackjack theory given in this book. Because of the extreme length of the data—there are enough final results alone to fill several books the size of this one with numbers—we limit ourselves to presenting complete-deck figures, and only an extract of these. Since in our discussion and application of these figures we generally do not need more than three decimal places, the tables given here are usually to three decimal places.

All figures are to be understood as having a decimal point on the left, though the decimal point is omitted. For example, −039 is to be read as −0.039.

We emphasize again that figures in this appendix were

computed assuming one complete deck and the rules of Chapter 3, including the rule of a dealer's soft standing number of 17. Since the figures may vary considerably if these conditions are altered, any deductions one makes on the basis of this appendix are precisely applicable only to the situation just described. Such deductions do, however, give rough insight into situations in which there are several decks in play or in which the rules are different.

In determining the player's strategy, the errors in our figures may cause errors, but only when the decision is very close. And in that case the errors caused by the erroneous strategy will be very small. This, plus the low frequency of close decisions, means the effect on the player's advantage of any strategic errors of this type are also very small. This is a virtue of the running count. Roughly speaking, certain close decisions, such as whether or not to draw on hard 16 when the dealer holds a Ten, will depend on what cards the player has drawn to make up his total of 16. For example, it is known that holding (*10,4,2*) the player should stand, while holding (*10,6*) he should draw. If several small cards have been drawn to make the total of 16, the decision may be fairly clear-cut. For example, if the cards drawn were (*4,4,4,4*), Julian Braun has shown that the player's *disadvantage* in drawing against a Ten is *precisely* (!) 6.382 per cent, as compared with the average player advantage of 2.9 per cent (3.2 per cent if (*8,8*) is split) in drawing to two-card hard 16 against a Ten.

One could attempt to improve the basic strategy by calculating the advantage or disadvantage of standing or drawing for each combination of cards the player can draw to make a total of hard 16. Then the player could consult a list of card combinations to see whether to draw or stand. This refinement, in all its precise detail, is impractical because its bulk (many hundreds of entries) would prevent the player from memorizing and using it in play. Furthermore, the net gain is quite small.

However, the running count in conjunction with the Tens strategy does take into account the cards the player draws. It is not as precise as the detailed strategy outlined above because it only classifies cards into two crude categories, Tens and others. But it does gain much—even most—of the difference.

TABLE 1. *Dealer's Probabilities.*

Dealer shows	Dealer's total					natural	busts
	17	18	19	20	21		
2	1390	1318	1318	1239	1205	......	3530
3	1303	1309	1238	1233	1160	......	3756
4	1310	1142	1207	1163	1151	......	4028
5	1197	1235	1169	1047	1063	......	4289
6	1670	1065	1072	1007	0979	......	4208
7	3723	1386	0773	0789	0730	......	2599
8	1309	3630	1294	0683	0698	......	2386
9	1219	1039	3574	1223	0611	......	2334
10	1144	1129	1147	3289	0365	0784	2143
A	1261	1310	1295	1316	0516	3137	1165
overall probability	1458	1381	1348	1758	0736	0483	2836

Table 1 gives the probability that the dealer will achieve a specified total for each possible value of his up card. The rows of the table do not generally quite add up to one because of small round-off and approximation errors. The defect is no more than 10^{-4} and so for practical purposes is negligible. The column totals show slight discrepancies with the overall probability figures because the original table had five figures and was rounded off *after* the columns were summed.

This table is of course valid only if we assume that the dealer plays all his hands out to a conclusion even though his opponents all bust. In an ordinary game the dealer does not do this.

From this point on, all tables are computed on the assumption that the dealer does not have a natural.

TABLE 2a. *Player's Gain by Drawing over Standing*
with Hard Totals

Dealer shows	Player's hard total								
	12	**13**	**14**	**15**	**16**	**17**	**18**	**19**	**20**
2	038	−016	−077	−141	−171	−383	−753	−1.135	−1.474
3	013	−045	−117	−179	−212	−417	−775	−1.096	−1.482
4	−017	−086	−158	−222	−258	−467	−761	−1.116	−1.491
5	−046	−117	−191	−260	−297	−448	−793	−1.157	−1.519
6	−025	−094	−167	−233	−220	−470	−853	−1.190	−1.542
7	209	166	114	119	110	−331	−957	−1.308	−1.608
8	189	148	145	108	102	−079	−657	−1.274	−1.626
9	141	145	103	062	055	−114	−400	−964	−1.586
10	156	119	075	038	029	−148	−471	−813	−1.420
A	246	221	186	159	146	−089	−554	−1.050	−1.533

To illustrate the use of Table 2a, suppose you have a hard total of 12 and the dealer shows a Two. If you decide to draw rather than stand, your gain is 0.038. This means that on the average over a large number of situations like this one, if you always draw rather than stand, with hard 12 against a Two, you will be better off by approximately an additional 3.8 per cent of your initial bet. If an entry is positive in the table, the player should draw rather than stand. Conversely, if an entry is negative the player should stand, not draw. The inspection of this table immediately yields the hard standing numbers. This is, in fact, how they were first obtained.

Similar remarks apply to Table 2b except that the entries yield the soft standing numbers.

There are two extremely close decisions, one each in Tables 2a and 2b. In Table 2a, the player who stands rather than draws on two-card hard 16 against a Ten loses, in these situations, an average amount of about 2.9 per cent of his wager. (With (*10,6*) the loss is 3.8 per cent, with (*9,7*) it is 0.8 per cent, and with (*8,8*) it is 0.9 per cent. Combining these numbers with weights 16:4:3 from probability theory gives 2.9 per cent. If (*8,8*) is split so that it is not included, the figure changes to 3.2 per cent.)

TABLE 2b. *Player's Gain by Drawing over Standing with Soft Totals.*

Dealer shows	Player's soft total			
	17	18	19	20
2	141	−072	−285	−470
3	132	−074	−251	−453
4	118	−048	−233	−430
5	141	−046	−236	−419
6	131	−067	−242	−418
7	152	−230	−388	−528
8	319	−071	−442	−608
9	270	092	−280	−660
10	233	045	−157	−547
A	291	−001	−303	−614

In Table 2b, the player who draws rather than stands on soft 18 against an Ace loses about 0.1 per cent in such situations. Some players I know of attempted to solve blackjack empirically; that is, they dealt out many hundreds or even thousands of hands and recorded results in an effort to decide which standing numbers were correct for various up cards of the dealer. As might be expected, these players were sharply divided on these two close decisions.

Table 3 was computed directly from Table 1 as follows. Suppose the player holds a given total, say 19, when the dealer's up card is a 6. The player's advantage is then the sum of the probabilities that the dealer will receive a poorer total (18, 17, or a bust), $0.1065 + 0.1670 + 0.4208 = 0.6943$, minus the probability that the dealer will have a better total (20 or 21), $0.1007 + 0.0979 = 0.1986$. The difference $0.6943 − 0.1986$ equals 0.4957, and rounding off to three significant figures we get 0.496, the entry in Table 3.

We are assuming in Table 3, as we said earlier, that the dealer does not have a natural. In this situation the player holding a natural always wins 1.5 times his original bet; that is, his advantage, in the sense that we are using the term, is 150 per cent. Thus there is no need to list that alternative in the table.

TABLE 3. *Player's Advantage Standing on Various Totals.*

Dealer shows	Player's total					
	16	17	18	19	20	21
2	−294	−155	116	379	635	879
3	−249	−119	143	397	644	884
4	−194	−063	182	417	653	885
5	−142	−023	221	461	683	894
6	−159	009	282	496	704	902
7	−480	−108	403	619	775	927
8	−523	−392	102	594	792	930
9	−533	−411	−185	276	756	939
10	−535	−411	−164	083	564	960
A	−660	−477	−102	278	658	925

Table 4 gives the player's advantage for all possible pairs of hole cards against a given up card of the dealer, assuming first that the player simply stands or draws using the proper standing numbers (deduced from Tables 2a and 2b). Then the player's advantage if he doubles down is given. Finally, the player's advantage is given for the cases in which his hole cards are numerically equal and he splits the pair and then does the most advantageous of the two alternatives of doubling down or drawing and standing. The table is divided into ten main sections, one for each value of the dealer's up card.

The basic strategy for each value of the dealer's up card can be deduced from the table as follows. First, suppose the hole cards form a pair. Compare the player's advantage from splitting the pair with his advantage from doubling down and from drawing. If it is greater than these, he should split. Otherwise he should do the more advantageous of doubling down and drawing or standing. For example, on holding (4,4) against a Ten, splitting gives an advantage of −0.552; doubling down gives an advantage of −0.739; and drawing and standing, using a hard standing number of 16 and a soft standing number of 19, gives an advantage of −0.241. Because this last figure is the best of the three, drawing and standing is the best alternative. Thus the player should not double down or split in this instance.

If the player's hole cards are $(A,2)$, this is the same as $(2,A)$; so only one of these two spots is filled in the table. Thus the subsections of Table 4 get their triangular shape.

Table 4 sheds further light on points about the basic strategy. In the discussion of pair splitting for the basic strategy, we say that if a pair of Aces is not split, the hand is "only fair for doubling down or drawing or standing," whereas splitting gives us a good chance for a winning hand. Table 4 gives us the precise advantage for the most profitable of the two alternatives of doubling down and drawing or standing. We see that the numbers waver around 0, with some positive and some negative. However the corresponding advantage for *splitting* the Aces is generally considerably positive, as shown by the table. Similarly, the rough oversimplification that the splitting of a pair of Eights against 7 through A breaks up a bad hand and replaces it by two average hands, is (only roughly) borne out by the table.

For the complete deck, Table 4 was used to compute the player's average advantage against various up cards of the dealer's and then the player's overall advantage was found. Similar results were obtained for the other decks from the appropriate data. The results are listed in Tables 4.1 and 9.2. They give some evidence of how much the various figures we give are affected when the deck composition or the rules vary.

TABLE 4a.†† *Dealer's Up Card Is Ten.*

Player's hole cards →	A	2	3	4	5	6	7	8	9	10
Drawing and standing										
A	−0470									
2	−0889	−2756								
3	−1236	−3078†	−3436†							
4	−1704	−3090	−3348	−2410						
5	−2234	−3451	−2509	−1381	0378					
6	−1887*	−2503*	−1411*	0344*	1133	−3866*				
7	−1387	−1541	0296	1096	−3846	−4503*	−5097**			
8	0643	0305*	1092	−3859	−4464	−4648	−4748	−5118*		
9	5546	1038	−3885	−3987	−4531	−5098*	−5120*	−3907	−1333	
10	1.5000	−3466	−3931	−4458	−5011	−5069*	−4123	−1552	1025	5832
Doubling down										
A	−4683									
2	−4790	−1.0943								
3	−4796	−1.0928	−1.0713							
4	−4963	−1.0731	−9555	−7390						
5	−5367	−9552	−7380	−4384	0180					
6	−4328	−7452	−4446	0112	1707	−8038				
7	−3213	−4355	0145	1710	−7906	−9083	−1.0347			
8	−2244	0060	1623	−8059	−9096	−9363	−9496	−1.0235		
9	−0520	1428	−8211	−8189	−9111	−1.0239	−1.0240	−1.1163	−1.2489	
10	1391	−7391	−8111	−8993	−1.0022	−1.0139	−1.1134	−1.2456	−1.4201	−1.6739
Pair Splitting	1942	−499	−498	−552	−648	−647	−606	−447	−265	033

MH=16   MS=19
*MH=17   †MS=18
**MH=14

†† MH = Minimum hard standing total
MS = Minimum soft standing total

TABLE 4b. *Dealer's Up Card Is Nine.*

Player's hole cards →	A	2	3	4	5	6	7	8	9	10
Drawing and standing										
A	−0027									
2	−0141	−2225								
3	−0600	−2625	−3100							
4	−1134*	−3046	−3039*	−2044*						
5	−1668	−2840*	−2171*	−0511*	1204*		MH=17	MS=19		
6	−1347	−2084	−0511	1174	1517	−3862	*MH=16			
7	−0870	−0524	1176	1495	−3896	−4185	−4746			
8	2880	1205	1392	−3949	−4134	−4372	−4432	−4871		
9	7656	1425	−3922	−3652	−4259	−4797	−4820	−4116	−1964	
10	1.5000	−3444	−3588	−4135	−4753	−4793	−4161	−1961	2643	7440
Doubling down										
A	−4206									
2	−3727	−1.0469								
3	−3935	−1.0659	−1.0653							
4	−4218	−1.0453	−9462	−7011						
5	−4520	−9263	−7029	−2790	1746					
6	−3452	−6916	−2897	1646	2399	−8174				
7	−2545	−2741	1537	2247	−8260	−8694	−9782			
8	−0602	1744	2152	−8337	−8476	−8879	−8936	−9742		
9	1105	2138	−8404	−7587	−8598	−9668	−9641	−1.0638	−1.1895	
10	2165	−7455	−7521	−8394	−9519	−9586	−1.0529	−1.1864	−1.3956	−1.6841
Pair Splitting	2898	−373	−395	−459	−560	−542	−535	−383	−093	172

TABLE 4c. *Dealer's Up Card Is Eight*

MH=17   MS=18

	Player's hole cards →	A	2	3	4	5	6	7	8	9	10
Drawing and standing	A	0930									
	2	0391	−1410								
	3	0350	−1808	−2311							
	4	−0355	−2342	−2284	−0548						
	5	−0843	−2178	−0570	1081	2075					
	6	−0649	−0559	1175	2075	2297	−3217				
	7	1209	1076	2171	2217	−3210	−3944	−4079			
	8	6078	2073	2203	−3192	−3868	−3691	−3796	−4263		
	9	7848	2153	−3161	−3389	−3701	−4207	−4278	−4149	0645	
	10	1.5000	−2745	−3282	−3574	−4180	−4248	−3942	0955	5768	7832
Doubling down	A	−2956									
	2	−3124	−1.0298								
	3	−2542	−1.0254	−9997							
	4	−3141	−1.0231	−8486	−4471						
	5	−3326	−8535	−4282	0007	3229					
	6	−2297	−4371	0142	3172	3657	−7114				
	7	−0153	0074	3269	3402	−7112	−8429	−8579			
	8	1902	2945	3300	−7193	−8291	−7746	−7774	−8526		
	9	2298	3277	−7037	−7241	−7619	−8556	−8556	−9506	−1.1325	
	10	3327	−6259	−7056	−7393	−8442	−8496	−8497	−1.1303	−1.3947	−1.6854
Pair Splitting		4065	−192	−244	−291	−391	−374	−378	−059	207	345

TABLE 4d. Dealer's Up Card Is Seven.

MH=17   MS=18

Player's hole cards →	A	2	3	4	5	6	7	8	9	10
Drawing and standing										
A	1584									
2	1073	-0918								
3	0604	-1192	-1645							
4	0337	-1639	-0706	1106						
5	-0238	-0674	0926	2013	2786					
6	0596	0918	1977	2856	2974	-2077				
7	4120	1836	2772	2938	-2582	-3307	-3892			
8	6145	2676	2918	-2456	-3275	-3485	-3241	-3736		
9	7732	2889	-2471	-2741	-3480	-3632	-3750	-1229	4011	
10	1.5000	-2120	-2704	-3422	-3645	-3762	-1213	3887	6101	7647
Doubling down										
A	-1370									
2	-1572	-9421								
3	-1745	-9378	-8712							
4	-1409	-8703	-5426	-1084						
5	-1891	-5672	-1323	1905	4663					
6	0142	-1481	1757	4754	5005	-5985				
7	2402	1600	4447	4874	-5852	-7141	-8230			
8	3253	4166	4726	-5636	-7065	-7346	-6660	-7471		
9	3513	4554	-5788	-6001	-7276	-7446	-7499	-8976	-1.1321	
10	4676	-4958	-5830	-7068	-7363	-7524	-9039	-1.1345	-1.3971	-1.6860
Pair Splitting	5×07	-006	-068	-160	-228	-228	-056	259	364	478

TABLE 4e. *Dealer's Up Card Is Six.*

MH=12   MS=18

Drawing and standing

Player's hole cards →	A	2	3	4	5	6	7	8	9	10
A	1996									
2	1685	0320								
3	1472	0192	0139							
4	1203	0141	0592	1753						
5	1159	0696	1637	2633	3618					
6	1332	1321	2313	3316	3807	−1652				
7	2622	2097	3180	3657	−1435	−1697	−1742			
8	4824	3075	3561	−1473	−1460	−1723	−1770	−1782		
9	6942	3458	−1538	−1514	−1501	−1765	−1796	−0114	2652	
10	1.5000	−1604	−1578	−1554	−1542	−1790	−0113	2681	4841	6974

Doubling down

Player's hole cards →	A	2	3	4	5	6	7	8	9	10
A	2479									
2	2302	−2490								
3	2218	−2438	−2145							
4	2007	−2150	−0569	1932						
5	2167	−0610	1899	4433	7236					
6	2665	1242	3792	6633	7614	−3871				
7	3849	3574	6361	7315	−3577	−5613	−7339			
8	4826	6151	7122	−3682	−5352	−6465	−7242	−7934		
9	5598	6916	−3876	−4563	−6175	−8018	−7944	−9676	−1.1734	
10	6822	−3189	−4578	−6162	−7746	−7926	−9667	−1.1722	−1.4140	−1.6900

Pair Splitting

	A	2	3	4	5	6	7	8	9	10
Pair Splitting	7583	240	220	183	131	151	220	356	437	543

TABLE 4f. Dealer's Up Card Is Five.

Player's hole cards →	A	2	3	4	5	6	7	8	9	10
Drawing and standing										
A	1820					MH=12	MS=18			
2	1587	0359								
3	1366	0215	0083							
4	1078	0089	0490	1539						
5	0821	0568	1411	2464	3473					
6	1400	1306	2350	3388	3936	−1022				
7	2223	1955	3075	3617	−1234	−1288	−1555			
8	4608	2960	3495	−1308	−1283	−1338	−1605	−1654		
9	6821	3398	−1368	−1339	−1314	−1369	−1636	−0444	2029	
10	1.5000	−1440	−1412	−1382	−1357	−1412	−0432	2023	4478	6737
Doubling down										
A	2157									
2	2123	−2140								
3	2036	−2085	−1840							
4	1750	−1855	−0614	1623						
5	1482	−0703	1550	4150	6947					
6	2800	1306	3916	6776	7873	−3247				
7	3491	3321	6150	7234	−3555	−5381	−7407			
8	4530	5920	6991	−3732	−5400	−6344	−7462	−9058		
9	5362	6796	−3932	−4641	−6277	−8041	−9041	−9852	−1.1806	
10	6630	−3271	−4706	−6293	−7992	−8884	−9849	−1.1815	−1.4175	−1.6912
Pair Splitting	7322	239	228	197	133	172	200	312	415	521

TABLE 4g. *Dealer's Up Card Is Four.*

Player's hole cards →	A	2	3	4	5	6	7	8	9	10
Drawing and standing										
A	1421									
2	1102	−0348					MH=12	MS=18		
3	0908	−0410	−0474							
4	0614	−0552	−0166	0978			MH=13			
5	0380	−0103	0866	1896	2949		*MH=13			
6	0773	0811	1860	2928	3520	−1519				
7	2040	1676	2852	3425	−1546	−1584	−1640			
8	4155	2525	3126	−1829	−1813	−1841	−1896	−2153		
9	6539	3000	−1913	−1885	−1859	−1886	−1942	−0844	1670	
10	1.5000	−1940*	−1971	−1934	−1907	−1935	−0644	1642	4041	6448
Doubling down										
A	1366									
2	1151	−3840								
3	1091	−3517	−3022							
4	0849	−3237	−1777	0441						
5	0626	−1946	0411	2970	5898					
6	1545	0233	2896	5855	7039	−3802				
7	3127	2718	5704	6851	−3836	−5541	−7376			
8	3731	5049	6252	−4281	−5836	−6751	−7601	−9223		
9	4592	6001	−4510	−5086	−6710	−8392	−9059	−1.0823	−1.1940	
10	5951	−3879	−5159	−6729	−8360	−9091	−1.0702	−1.1946	−1.4234	−1.6926
Pair Splitting	6686	112	102	076	014	047	103	215	320	444

TABLE 4h. Dealer's Up Card Is Three.

Player's hole cards →

Drawing and standing

	A	2	3	4	5	6	7	8	9	10
A	1203									
2	0705	-0818								
3	0442*	-0983	-1182							
4	0234*	-1062*	-0815*	0288*						
5	-0019*	-0615*	0194*	1411*	2548*					
6	0369*	0238*	1389*	2504	3147*	-2111*				
7	1668	1308	2461*	3056*	-2124*	-2148	-2194			
8	4198	2412*	2952*	-2202*	-2167	-2202	-2239	-2284		
9	6441	2690*	-2557	-2460	-2436	-2460	-2497	-1207	1225	
10	1.5000	-2193	-2657	-2509	-2474	-2499	-1190	1444	3835	6361

Notes (in upper region): MH=13   MS=18   *MH=12   MH=12

Doubling down

	A	2	3	4	5	6	7	8	9	10
A	0549									
2	0284	-5015								
3	0108	-4970	-4721							
4	0026	-4455	-3237	-0825						
5	-0192	-3107	-0832	1956	5096					
6	0739	-0783	1892	5009	6294	-4443				
7	1889	1946	4921	6111	-4439	-6081	-7765			
8	3460	4825	5904	-4595	-6112	-6939	-7626	-8999		
9	3922	5380	-5114	-5607	-7121	-8646	-9180	-1.0710	-1.2766	
10	5363	-4386	-5664	-7114	-8595	-9228	-1.0728	-1.2673	-1.4251	-1.6926

Pair Splitting

	A	2	3	4	5	6	7	8	9	10
	8219	020	-031	-048	-104	-069	-020	132	242	383

TABLE 4i. *Dealer's Up Card Is Two.*

Player's hole cards →	A	2	3	4	5	6	7	8	9	10
Drawing and standing										
A	0948									
2	0392	−1132								
3	0169	−1314	−1530							
4	−0117	−1507	−1230	−0126						
5	−0317	−0994	−0165	0933	2238					
6	0071	−0130	0921	2175	2840	−2527				
7	1358	0835	2144	2723	−2526	−2651	−2684			
8	4016	2130	2682	−2598	−2650	−2679	−2721	−2749		
9	6559	2636	−2663	−2858	−2694	−2734	−2766	−1366	1370	
10	1.5000	−2434*	−3042*	−3102	−2948	−2977	−1582	1188	3848	6272
Doubling down										
A	−0193									
2	−0420	−5816								
3	−0468	−5866	−5675							
4	−0700	−5602	−4291	−1846						
5	−0819	−4018	−1678	1135	4464					
6	0133	−1628	1118	4322	5672	−5054				
7	1276	1174	4260	5417	−5053	−6639	−8128			
8	2372	4245	5336	−5197	−6626	−7252	−7808	−9082		
9	3798	5248	−5325	−5860	−7179	−8605	−9120	−1.0603	−1.2550	
10	4870	−4868	−6084	−7376	−8724	−9308	−1.0769	−1.2651	−1.4993	−1.6933
Pair Splitting	5657	−047	−116	−156	−193	−165	−105	064	188	331

MH=13   MS=18
*MH=14

TABLE 4j. Dealer's Up Card Is Ace.

Player's hole cards →	A	2	3	4	5	6	7	8	9	10
Drawing and standing										
A	−0307						MH=17	MS=18		
2	−0678	−2589						*MS=19		
3	−1006	−2916	−3340							
4	−1539	−3349	−3450	−2090						
5	−2061	−3311	−2171	−0702	0906					
6	−1999*	−2258	−0785	0815	1729	−3862				
7	−1010	−0828	0868	1713	−3768	−4434	−4947			
8	2897	0864	1709	−3749	−4330	−4534	−4557	−4949		
9	6807	1696	−3745	−3831	−4412	−4958	−4955	−4519	−0552	
10	1.5000	−3489	−3925	−4450	−4987	−5088	−4670	−0820	3077	6501
Doubling down										
A	−5988									
2	−5933	−1.3201								
3	−5958	−1.3188	−1.2982							
4	−6199	−1.2957	−1.1264	−1.2982						
5	−6561	−1.1252	−7940	−1.1264	0551					
6	−5272	−7991	−4013	0486	2402	−8346				
7	−3578	−4021	0402	2220	−8375	−9372	−1.0294			
8	−1921	0251	2057	−8467	−9309	−9418	−9280	−9898		
9	−0407	1889	−8582	−8380	−9206	−1.0084	−9910	−1.0892	−1.2497	
10	1452	−8109	−8590	−9316	−1.0129	−1.0175	−1.1116	−1.2664	−1.4853	−1.7664
Pair Splitting	2239	−422	−465	−527	−613	−617	−613	−363	−113	097

References

[1] ASHBAUGH, DON, "Game for Gaming," *Las Vegas Review Journal* (Sunday Feature Section), December 25, 1960, pp. 20, 22.

[2] BALDWIN, ROGER; CANTEY, WILBERT; MAISEL, HERBERT; and McDERMOTT, JAMES, "The Optimum Strategy in Blackjack," *Journal of the American Statistical Association*, Vol. 51, 429–439 (1956).

[3] ———, *Playing Blackjack to Win; A New Strategy for the Game of 21* (M. Barrows & Co., Inc., New York, 1957).

[4] *Boston Globe*, January 24, 1961, pp. 1, 11.

[5] CARDANO, GEROLAMO, *Book on Games of Chance* (written about 1520 and first published in 1663). Translated by SIDNEY H. GOULD (Holt, Rinehart and Winston, Inc., New York and San Francisco, 1961).

[6] *Columbus Dispatch*, January 30, 1961, p. 1-B.

[7] COOTNER, PAUL H., ed., *The Random Character of Stock Prices* (M. I. T. Press, Cambridge, Massachusetts).

[8] CRAWFORD, JOHN R., *How to Be a Consistent Winner in the Most Popular Card Games* (Doubleday and Co., Inc., New York, 1953).

[9] CULBERTSON, ELY; MOREHEAD, ALBERT; MOTT-SMITH, GEOFFREY, *Culbertson's Card Games Complete, with Official Rules* (The Greystone Press, New York, 1952).

[10] DARVAS, NICHOLAS, *Wall Street, The Second Las Vegas* (Stuart, Lyle, New York, 1962).

[11] FELLER, WILLIAM, *An Introduction to Probability Theory and Its Applications*, Vol. I, Second Edition (John Wiley & Sons, Inc., New York, 1957).

[12] FOX, PHILLIP G. (as told to STANLEY FOX), "A Primer for Chumps," *Saturday Evening Post*, November 21, 1959, pp. 31ff.

[13] FREY, RICHARD L., *According to Hoyle* (Fawcett Publications, Inc., Greenwich, Conn., 1956).

[14] FURST, DOCTOR BRUNO, *The Practical Way to a Better Memory* (Fawcett Publications, Inc., Greenwich, Conn., 1957).

[15] GARCIA, FRANK, *Marked Cards and Loaded Dice* (Prentice-Hall, Inc., New York, 1962).

[16] GOODMAN, MIKE, *How to Win at Cards, Dice, Races and Roulette* (Holloway House Publishing Co., Los Angeles, 1963).

[17] GREENSPUN, HANK, "Where I Stand," *Las Vegas Sun*, January 26, 1962, p. 1.

[18] HUFF, DARRELL, *The Mathematics of Sex, Gambling and Insurance* (Harper & Brothers, New York, 1959).

[19] JONES, JACK, *Golden Nugget Gaming Guide* (Silver State Publishing Co., Las Vegas, 1949).

[20] JONES, STRAT (AP), "Thorp's Book Brings About Vegas Shakeup," *Las Cruces Sun-News*, April 3, 1964, p. 1.

[21] KATCHER, LEO, *The Big Bankroll; the Life and Times of Arnold Rothstein* (Harper & Brothers, New York, 1959).

[22] K. C. Card Co., *Forty-second Anniversary Blue Book*, 1960, Chicago, 1959.

[23] KELLY, J. L., "A New Interpretation of Information Rate," *IRE Transactions on Information Theory*, Vol. IT-2, No. 3, September, 1956. *Bell System Tech. J.*, Vol. 35, 917–926 (1956).

[24] *Las Cruces Sun-News*, "Mobster Swears Gang Boss Has Interests in Las Vegas," October 1, 1963, p. 1.

[25] *Las Vegas Review-Journal*, "Silver Slipper Raided," April 4, 1964, p. 1.

[26] *Las Vegas Review-Journal*, "State Casinos Change Rules on '21' Games," April 2, 1964, p. 1.

[27] *Las Vegas Sun*, January 25 and 27, 1961.

[28] *Las Vegas Sun*, "U.S. to Smash Mob-Ruled LV Casinos," January 29, 1962, p. 1.

[29] LEWIS, OSCAR, *Sagebrush Casinos: The Story of Legal Gambling in Nevada* (Doubleday & Co., Inc., New York, 1953).

[30] *Life*, "Senators Survey Low-Belly Strippers," September 1, 1961, p. 39.

[31] *Los Angeles Herald Examiner*, "Can YOU Beat Blackjack?" June 10, 1962, p. H1.

[32] *Los Angeles Herald Examiner*, "Crooked Dice Charge; Vegas Casino Closed. First Case of Cheating in Nevada (*sic*)," April 4, 1964, p. 1.

[33] *Los Angeles Times*, "Federal Extortion Case May Link Las Vegas Gambling to Underworld," February 6, 1964, p. 1.

[34] *Los Angeles Times*, "Vegas Casinos Cry Uncle, Change Rules," April 2, 1964.

[35] MACDOUGALL, MICHAEL, "Even 'Honest' Vegas House Cheats," *Sunday Star-Ledger*, Newark, New Jersey, December 2, 1962, p. 35.

[36] ———, *MacDougall on Dice and Cards* (Coward-McCann, Inc., New York, 1944).

[37] ———, "Nevada Trumps a Blackjack Dealer," *Sunday Star-Ledger*, Newark, New Jersey, April 19, 1964, section 2, p. 2.

[38] MCKINSEY, JOHN C., *Introduction to the Theory of Games* (McGraw-Hill Book Co., Inc., New York, 1952).

[39] *Miami News*, January 25, 1961, p. 6A.

[40] MONROE, KEITH, "William Harrah: The New Gambling King, and the Social Scientists," *Harper's*, January, 1962.

[41] *The Nation*, February 4, 1961.

[42] *Newsweek*, "Gambling: Hello Suckers," September 4, 1961, pp. 22ff.

[43] *New York Herald Tribune*, January 29, 1961, pp. 1, 24.

[44] *New York Journal American*, "Computer Beats House at '21' in Las Vegas," November 15, 1963, p. 1.

[45] *New York Journal American*, "How Wizard of Odds Beat Las Vegas Cards," April 3, 1964, p. 1.

[46] *New York Times*, Western Edition, "Las Vegas: Gambling Take Creates New Force in U. S.; Millions in Untaxed 'Black Money' Give Obscure Figures Power that Extends from Underworld to Government," November 18, 1963.

[47] *New York Times Book Review*, Best Seller List, April 19 and May 3.

[48] OLSEN, ED, Letter to the Editor, *Life*, April 17, 1964, p. 27.

[49] O'NEIL, PAUL, "The Professor Who Breaks the Bank," *Life*, March 27, 1964, pp. 80–91.

[50] ORE, OYSTEIN, *Cardano, The Gambling Scholar* [with a trans-

lation (from the Latin of Cardano's book, *Games of Chance*) by SIDNEY HENRY GOULD] (Princeton University Press, Princeton, N. J., 1953).

[51] *Parade Sunday Magazine*, Intelligence Report: "Crimes," August 25, 1963.

[52] POINCARÉ, HENRI, *Science and Method*. Translated by Francis Maitland (Dover Publications, Inc., New York, 1958).

[53] RADNER, SIDNEY H., *How to Spot Card Sharps and Their Methods* (Key Publishing Co., New York, 1957).

[54] THE RAND CORPORATION, *A Million Random Digits with 100,000 Normal Deviates* (Free Press of Glencoe, Illinois, 1955).

[55] REID, ED and DEMARIS, OVID, *The Green Felt Jungle* (Trident, New York, 1963). Reprinted and enlarged (Pocket Books, Inc., New York, 1964). All references are to the enlarged Pocket Book version.

[56] RIDDLE, MAJOR A., as told to Hyams, Joe, *The Weekend Gambler's Handbook* (Random House, New York, 1963).

[57] ROBB, INEZ, "Bets Are Off," *New York World-Telegram and Sun*, February 7, 1961.

[58] SCARNE, JOHN, *Scarne's Complete Guide to Gambling* (Simon and Shuster, Inc., New York, 1961).

[59] SCHERMAN, DAVID E., "It's Bye! Bye! Blackjack," *Sports Illustrated*, January 13, 1964.

[60] SCIENTIFIC AMERICAN, "How to Beat the Game," April, 1961, p. 84.

[61] SHEINWOLD, ALFRED, "It's in the Cards: Blackjack—Counting the Cards," *Argosy*, August, 1961.

[62] SHERMAN, GENE, "'Off The Top' Plagues Gambling Authorities. Pocketing Money Without Being Reported for Tax Purposes Called Impossible to Prove," *Los Angeles Times*, October 28, 1963.

[63] Showboat Hotel, Las Vegas, Nevada, "The Univac '21' Formula for Standing or Drawing."

[64] SMITH, HAROLD S., *I Want to Quit Winners* (Prentice Hall, Englewood Cliffs, New Jersey, 1961).

[65] *Sports Illustrated*, "Calculated Risk," February 6, 1961, pp. 4, 5.

[66] STEEN, JOAN, "Exposing Crooked Gambler's Tricks," *Popular Science Monthly*, January, 1962, pp. 61ff.

[67] THORP, EDWARD O., "Fortune's Formula: The Game of Blackjack," *Notices of the American Mathematical Society*, December, 1960, pp. 935–936.

[68] ———, "A Favorable Strategy for Twenty-One," *Proceedings of the National Academy of Sciences,* Vol. 47, No. 1, pp. 110–112 (1961).

[69] ———, "A Prof Beats the Gamblers," *The Atlantic Monthly,* June, 1962.

[70] ——— and WALDEN, W., A Winning Bet in Nevada Baccarat, 70+ pp., lecture notes, 1964 (out of print).

[71] *Time,* Modern Living: "Eight Days to Win," January 13, 1961, p. 82ff.

[72] *Time,* "Games: 'Beating the Dealer,'" January 25, 1963, p. 70.

[73] *Time,* Non-Fiction Best Seller List, May 29, 1964, p. 4.

[74] TURNER, WALLACE, "Nevada Gambling Faces New Test," *New York Times,* April 12, 1964, p. 53.

[75] ———, *New York Times.* November 18, 1963 to November 22, 1963, p. 1.

[76] WALDEN, W., Ph.D. Thesis, New Mexico State University (unpublished).

[77] WANNISKI, JUDE, "Gamblers Shuffle Blackjack Rules Back to Old Deal," *The National Observer,* June 15, 1964, p. 8.

[78] *Washington Post and Times Herald,* January 25, 1961, p. 3; editorial, "High Stakes," p. A16, January 26, 1961.

[79] WILLIAMS, JOHN D., *The Compleat Strategyst* (McGraw-Hill Book Co., Inc., New York, 1954).

[80] WILSON, ALLAN, *The Casino Gambler's Guide* (Harper and Row, New York, 1965).

List of Figures and Tables

Index[*]

[*] fn denotes that the particular item may be found in a footnote on the given page.

ABOUT THE AUTHOR

EDWARD O. THORP is currently teaching at the Irvine campus of the University of California, where he is an Associate Professor of Mathematics. Prior to this he taught at New Mexico State University. Professor Thorp was also a C.L.E. Moore instructor at the Massachusetts Institute of Technology, and he taught at the University of California at Los Angeles, from which he received a Ph.D. in 1958. Professor Thorp is a member of the American Mathematical Society and of Phi Beta Kappa. Professor Thorp's major fields of interest include probability and game theory. He is the author of a text in probability theory and of numerous articles, both in learned journals and in popular magazines.